THE
CONFIDENCE
BOOK

**75 Ways to Reduce Your Anxiety,
Let Go of Your Fears, Change Your
Negative Thinking, and
Perform at Your Professional Best**

ALSO BY GARY GENARD

NONFICTION

How to Give a Speech
(Second Expanded Edition)

Fearless Speaking: Beat Your Anxiety,
Build Your Confidence, Change Your Life

Speaking Virtually

Speak for Leadership

THE DR. WILLIAM SCARLET MYSTERIES

Red Season

Year of the Rippers

The Master of Illusion

The Way to Dusty Death

THE
CONFIDENCE
BOOK

75 Ways to Reduce Your Anxiety,
Let Go of Your Fears, Change Your
Negative Thinking, and
Perform at Your Professional Best

GARY GENARD

Cedar &
Maitland
Press

The Genard Method
1337 Massachusetts Avenue, Suite 237
Arlington, MA 02476

www.genardmethod.com
info@genardmethod.com
(617) 993-3410
Author website: www.garygenard.com

First Edition

Cover design: Yesna99
Book interior formatting: TeaBerryStudio.com

ISBN: 979-8-9918975-2-5 (paperback)
ISBN: 979-8-9918975-3-2 (ebook)
Library of Congress Control Number: 2025912226

Printed in the United States of America

To order this book, please call (617) 993-3410,
or contact info@genardmethod.com.
Group and academic discounts are available.

Visit our website at www.genardmethod.com

Dedicated to you, dear reader—the only one
who can make you truly confident.

Contents

Acknowledgment

Grateful acknowledgment is made to reprint in Chapter 5 the mindfulness exercises from:

> *The Miracle of Mindfulness* by Thich Nhat Hanh
> Copyright © 1975, 1976 by Thich Nhat Hanh
> Preface and English translation Copyright ©
> 1975, 1976, 1987 by Mobi Ho
> Reprinted by permission of Beacon
> Press, Boston

The Person You Show the World

First keep the peace within yourself, then you
can also bring peace to others.
— Thomas à Kempis, *Imitation of Christ* (1420)

You gain strength, courage and confidence by
every experience in which you really stop to look
fear in the face. You are able to say to yourself,
"I lived through this...I can take the next thing
that comes along."
— Eleanor Roosevelt, *You Learn By Living* (1960)

Are you ready to show yourself to the world?

Well, of course you are! You've been doing it every single day
of your life.

Ah...but *which you*? The happy, confident, personable one?
That "you" is everything you want it to be: competent, likable,
intelligent (perhaps funny?), responsible, loving, empathetic,
effective...and making a difference in the world.

That's the you this book intends to help you show to others.

The problem, of course, is that you're human—which means that like everyone else on the planet, part of your burden includes doubts, insecurities, fears, and past failures. It doesn't matter if you're a generally anxious person or someone whom others think of as a classic Type A personality—you still have to deal with these personal demons.

For instance, in my work as an actor, confidence coach and expert in performance-based speech training, I work with many high-level professionals who still find themselves (sometimes after many successful years in their profession), suddenly struggling with self-doubt and even panic attacks. One of the insights I've gained over twenty-five years of work in this field is that this "slippage" of confidence isn't as sudden or as related to one area of performance as the person dealing with the problem thinks it is.

In other words, it's always part of what's going on in that person's life *as a whole*. Most of the time, things have started to change in their personal life, professional life, or both. These changes may have been going on for some time, but often they are pushed aside or ignored. When that happens, insecurities and fears can seem to reveal themselves all at once, in a straw-that-broke-the-camel's-back moment. It isn't the moment itself that causes the break; it's simply the accumulation of some powerful forces that have been impinging on that person's well-being for some time. Those forces just happen to reveal themselves fully in that moment, so that they come starkly into view. What can happen then is that the safe and sturdy structure the person believed they were living inside suddenly seems to crumble.

Whether you're dealing with a sudden realization of your own challenges like this, or have been working steadily for some time to reduce your anxieties and fears, there's good news. Tried-and-true strategies, tactics, and approaches exist to *get you back on track*. They are the exercises you will find in this book. There are two ways to think of this: (a) *reviving a once strong but now weakened level of self-belief*, or (b) *gaining a new level of confidence*. Either way, the approaches and exercises you'll find in these pages will lead the way toward a newly confident you.

ABOUT THIS BOOK

The Confidence Book is written according to a simple but powerful formula. It is a holistic approach to making you a more confident and less anxious person. Importantly, that includes the ability *to know how to continually enhance your confidence*, along with your comfort level around others, and the knowledge of how to succeed when dealing with them.

It is meant for people from all walks of life, and is unrelated to your job or profession or anything else about you that's very specific. If you're human, you deal with the same doubts and insecurities that all of us do. Like everyone else, you're faced with the issues involved in dealing with other people who have complex personalities, just like you. And wherever you live and whatever your lifestyle, chances are you struggle to keep up with the many demands of your time and would like to find a quick and reliable way to relax. That, too, is in these pages.

The seventy-five exercises in *The Confidence Book* will help you in four specific areas: (1) calming your nerves and learning to relax; (2) reducing your anxiety and fears; (3) becoming a more confident individual; and (4) improving your success in social and business situations.

Some of the exercises you'll be doing are taken from some of my other books, including *How to Give a Speech*, *Fearless Speaking*, and *Speak for Leadership*. The difference is that those books are wholly concerned with public speaking improvement. This book offers a wider application of the approaches and exercises that have shown themselves to be tried and true ways for you to become a less anxious and fearful person. At the same time, they will help you gain self-confidence while learning how to live fully in the moment.

THE TWELVE KEY AREAS OF FOCUS

There are twelve key areas of focus we're going to discover and practice together in the pages ahead. Here they are:

1. Relaxation exercises
2. Breathing techniques
3. The brain's role in fear and anxiety
4. Body awareness
5. Practicing mindfulness to live fully in the moment
6. Cognitive restructuring to change your negative thinking
7. Using positive visualization
8. Biofeedback
9. Body language and nonverbal communication
10. Vocal dynamics and voice improvement
11. Improving your social and business interactions
12. Awareness of and implementing your brand

Are You Ready To Show The World Your Best Face? For all of us, the things we say and do and the way we relate to other people make up "the face we show the world." It's much more than the way we dress or groom ourselves, or the social standing we possess. And it goes far beyond the level of knowledge and professionalism we display.

This image or brand is important for two reasons. First, of course, it affects how people perceive you, judge you, and make decisions about you, including what they think about your personality, abilities, and intentions. And that affects how they *feel* about you, and whether they want to be around you! That's all part of the first reason. The second is, you yourself are strongly affected by your own perceptions about how people perceive you and how *you* feel about yourself.

Consider the difference in the way you feel when you're nicely turned out and on your way to an exciting social event, versus when you've just thrown some clothes on and know you're a mess but you just had to make a quick stop at the grocery store before you started getting ready and…oops! you just had to run into *her* or *him (or them)!*

Of course it's true that *confidence breeds confidence.* If you act and carry yourself confidently—if you broadcast confidence— the feedback loop is a reliable one: those you interact with will also have confidence in you. Sometimes, however, it's simply a case of fake-it-till-you-make-it. At these times, you may not have the luxury of *being* confident, so much as you have to *appear* so. (See Exercise 47 for help with that one.) There are simply times when you need to get others to be confident about you, by hook or by crook.

But there's no need for you to worry about that right now. The pages that follow are meant to *actually* make you less anxious, more relaxed, not as fearful, and above all, on the path to developing a genuinely more confident *you*, not just making it seem that way.

Let's get started.

CHAPTER 1

Calming Your Nerves and Relaxing the Body

Exercise 1: Stop — Breathe — Listen

We begin with a habit that's essential for facing the world as a relaxed and confident individual: living in the present moment.

Are you doing that now? Are you mindful of the world as it is happening, moment by moment, while being aware of your part in it? Or are you like most of us, hurrying from task to task so that you can get to the *next* task?

This isn't just a modern phenomenon—though it's much worse than in centuries past. People throughout history have been juggling busy and challenging lives. But there's something about 21st-century society that *demands* that we split our focus, and therefore our effectiveness in responding to the environment around us.

Take cell phones.

Dumb, flip, smart, or stuffed with AI—it doesn't matter.

These computers-in-our-pockets are turning us into digitized slaves and zombies. And of course, they are only *one* of the tools that are pulling us away from the here-and-now. I'm sure you can name a ton of others from your own personal and professional lives.

I mention cell phones because lately I've been observing some new behavior. I'll bet you have, too. Some delivery people (and even, I'm sorry to say, floor help and cashiers in retail establishments), can't seem to do their job without at the same time having a private conversation on their cell phone. This amazes me. While I'm working in my home office, say, I'll hear someone talking loudly outside (as people do in cell phone conversations). I know enough by now to say to myself, "Ah, that must be the mail deliverer, or the guy from Amazon or FedEx or UPS." Are sure enough, a few seconds later I'll hear the clank of my mailbox or the sound of a package being dropped onto the front porch or placed between the doors of my house.

The reason this seems strange to me, is that multitasking is a surefire way to split your focus and efficiency and diminish your ability to attend to the job at hand. Not to mention your relationship with the *other* parts of the equation. Other people, for instance. Think of how you feel when someone is, say, scrolling through their cell phone messages while having a conversation with you.

Yet nowadays, having a personal conversation on your cell phone while performing the job you're being paid for seems to have become almost the new norm overnight! (Oh, I forgot to mention cab and ride-share drivers. Doesn't that make that person's driving dangerous?)

Of course, the problem isn't the phone. It's us. Take the cells out of the mix and it's exactly the same. We're the ones who are *choosing* to disrupt our response to the world and to the moment. And we do it all the time. So, if you want to show the world a person who is relaxed, confident, caring, attentive, and at ease with others, you need to be a focused and responsible user of the entity you have and are—yourself.

Just like me and everybody else, you need to start paying more attention to the world around you, moment by moment.

That's why the very first directive in this book is STOP.

Doing this simple thing is a hugely important act if you are starting to feel anxious, are becoming fearful, or are sensing that you're not connecting with others around you. It's important that you put the brakes on what's happening before things start to speed up and it becomes that much more difficult for you to take charge of your response.

But it also matters just generally, in terms of how you're living your everyday life. Every moment of every day, there are things trying to pull you away from being focused and mindful. What are some of them? The breakneck speed of computer-based applications. Our over-scheduled lives: work, family, and personal. The 24-hour news cycles. (How about channels that have people talking to the camera while a *separate* news feed is scrolling across the bottom of the screen?) The beeps of mail or text messages coming in like tiny missiles. The constantly decreasing sound bites on news shows, demanding that we stop thinking about that, and go on to *this*. The ever-shortening camera shots and quick-takes in movies and commercials, substituting noise and movement for anything of value.

It has become so much a part of our lives, that it now may feel odd to take the time to stop the constant spinning of our minds and contemplate this moment in time. We're out of practice.

So, stop.

Now breathe.

Breathing slowly and deeply tells the brain and adrenal glands to stop sending out adrenaline: the "fight-or-flight" response. It is the perfect way to bring yourself back into the here-and-now. Your very first breath was your initial moment of life outside the womb. It's still the best tool you have for bringing yourself back into the world, from wherever you were a moment ago in your frenzied response to the whirlwind around you. When you focus on your breathing, you *can't* be anywhere but in the present.

Next, listen. Listen to the sounds around you, of course. But I actually mean more than that. Listen with your whole being—take everything in with all of your senses. Become an open vessel. You're hearing and seeing things; but you're also taking in a whole universe of sensations: the air on your skin, the smell of the environment around you, the sensation of your feet on the ground or floor and the positions of different parts of your body. The air you're breathing is refreshing and delicious. Taste it! Now go one step further in terms of your awareness, feeling how that inhaled breath moves down your throat and into your lungs, then out to every cell in your body.

You can do these three things—stop, breathe, and listen—for as short or long a time as you want, however many times a day you'd like. Take a few seconds to bring yourself back into the reality of the moment, or fifteen minutes if you can find a quiet place to relax and you'd like to connect with yourself before you reconnect with the world.

It's amazing how much is happening within you AND without you when you make the effort to make nothing happen!

Exercise 2: Got 10 Minutes? — Relax!

"Easy does it."

"Take it easy."

"Easy as pie."

We admire people who not only do things expertly, but who make them seem easy.

I believe one of the reasons we feel this way, is that when things are going smoothly—when we're hitting on all cylinders— we're functioning at peak efficiency. And that just feels *right.*

Some people call this level of performance achieving "flow," or being in The Zone. Whatever name you attach to it, it's a feeling of effortlessness—an intense pleasure that comes from focusing completely on the task at hand rather than the obstacles in your way.

Of course, you can't really do this unless you're relaxed and available for that task. I call this getting to a state of *natural relaxation.* Once you're there, you can place your focus where it needs to be: on whatever you're being called upon to do.

But given your probably demanding work schedule and per- sonal obligations, you probably also need a way to help you relax *quickly.* So here's a wonderful way to achieve a productive level of relaxation (yes, there is such a thing!) if you only have 10 minutes to spare. As an added benefit, you'll "charge yourself up" at the end to introduce energy into your relaxed state. That way, you'll experience the best of both worlds: a relaxed *and* energized state.

And it will only take you 10 minutes.

I'm grateful to my dear friend and colleague Jeannie Lindheim for allowing me to use the exercise below. It's from her book *Trusting the Moment*, and it's called "Liquid."

- Lie down on a yoga mat, carpet, or other soft surface, with your feet uncrossed and hands at your sides. Imagine a liquid is being poured into the top of your head. Be aware of the liquid's color, thickness, and texture as it fills up the inside of your head.

- It's a very pleasant feeling as the liquid now flows down through your head and into your neck and shoulders. It continues flowing downward through your arms, relaxing each arm completely. Let some of the liquid trickle out through your fingers.

- The rest of the liquid goes slowly down into your chest and waist, hips and thighs. It continues down through the inside of your body, relaxing each part it touches. It flows into your calves and feet and dribbles out slowly through your toes.

- At this point, the liquid magically gathers on the floor underneath you and begins pouring in again through the top of your head. This time, go more slowly as you imagine (feel) the sensations. Allow the liquid to flow downward at your own pace, letting it relax each part of your body it touches. Let the liquid create small pools where you continue to feel any pockets of tension. Then, once it has allowed that tension to melt away, allow it to continue downward as before.

- Now, become aware of your BREATH going in and out. Visualize the oxygen that in its turn is flowing downward into you. Your body begins to feel very light, as if it were floating on a piece of chiffon. Or if you prefer, let your body suddenly feel very heavy as if it was sinking into the ground. Either visualization works to make you more body aware.

- **Sitting Position and Standing Up:** When you're ready, slowly sit up. Do this by rolling over onto your side in a prenatal position and then slowly sitting up. Use the least amount of effort possible. Now slowly stand, taking your time.

- **Energy**: Once you're standing, feel the energy coming up through the earth and into you through the soles of your feet. This automatically happens once you're "grounded" to the earth. The feeling of energy starts slowly and then builds, radiating upward into your feet and legs, then your chest, and eventually into your head. (This of course is the opposite direction of the "liquid" that flowed downward through your body.) But don't let this magnificent energy-from-the-earth escape out of the top of your head! Keep it contained and controlled: an ongoing source of power that swirls within you. In fact, there is an aura around you now that is radiating outward until it fills the whole room and goes beyond even that. You are luminous: a source of strength and light. Slowly open your eyes and continue your day in this state.

Exercise 3: Body Over Mind: The Progressive Relaxation Exercise

Here's another exercise that will help you achieve a state of complete relaxation. Like the previous exercise, it involves visualization. This time, however, you'll focus a bit more on releasing muscular tension throughout your body. This will also make it much easier for you to practice relaxed breathing, which is the focus of the next chapter.

Once again, do this exercise while lying on a yoga mat or carpet. The first time you practice the sequence it may take up to twenty minutes to reach the state of relaxation described. With more practice, it might take you only ten minutes to achieve the same state of full mental and physical relaxation.

- Lie on your back, with eyes closed and arms and feet uncrossed at your sides.

- Follow your breath: Be aware of breathing in and out easily. Visualize your breath as it enters your mouth or nose and goes down your throat. Stay with the nourishing breath, visualizing it passing into your lungs and then throughout your body. Sense how the oxygen nourishes every cell in your body. Become conscious of how refreshing and life-affirming each miraculous breath is.

- Now, as you continue to breathe easily, as in the previous exercise focus your awareness on the top of your head. This time, however, you're after a sense of complete relaxation up there: as you concentrate on that area, your scalp and the individual hairs on your head suddenly *release* all tension held within them. A pleasantly heavy sensation like warm lava is spreading across your scalp, gently melting away all tension as it moves.

- Once your scalp is covered with this warm, heavy feeling, allow it to spread downward onto your forehead. Feel the same release of tension in the forehead—the melting-away, the sensation of smoothness and relaxation where once there might have been tightness.

- Keeping the level of relaxation you've achieved in your scalp and forehead, let the lava keep flowing downward until it covers your eyes. You may hold considerable tension behind your eyes—many people do. Let that tension now melt away.

- At your own pace, allow the warm melting-lava feeling to *slowly* proceed down the rest of your body. Each part of your body that it reaches immediately relaxes, as all tension there disappears. When you get to your fingers, allow any remaining tension to flow out your fingertips. And when you get to your feet, let the same thing happen through your toes. Don't DO anything; just let it happen.

- Once your *entire body* is completely relaxed, do a mental scan to locate any remaining pockets of tension. Then focus for a moment on each of those areas, letting the tightness there vanish until you're completely and utterly relaxed there as well.

- **AN IMPORTANT PART OF THIS EXERCISE:** Allow your *muscles*—not your intellect—to remember what this sensation of complete body relaxation feels like. Register it not in your mind but in your muscle memory.

- Now that you're utterly relaxed, and while still lying down, place the palm of your dominant hand on your abdomen where it rises and falls with each breath. Breathe gently and deeply. Feel your hand moving up and down with the "bellows" action of your diaphragm. This is what natural breathing in a relaxed state feels like.

Exercise 4: Melissa Learns to Feel More Like Herself

"When I present, I know I'm being judged," Melissa told me at our first meeting. More revealing was her next comment: "I'm just not emotionally connected with my audience. I'm protected by my designs, you see—I go into a zone when I speak and don't connect with people."

Melissa designs jewelry for a home shopping network, and she frequently showcases her work. She is very secure about the high quality of her designs. But she found that she was uncomfortable talking to others about the products and selling her ideas and vision. Consequently, she had no confidence in her ability to adequately represent her wares in these make-or-break pitches. She felt like she was on autopilot—almost as if she didn't need to be there. In fact, she once said of her work: "The designs should sell themselves."

Melissa's problem was *presence,* for she was never really in the present moment during her televised conversations with prospective customers and clients. She would speak quickly, giving almost all of her attention to the larger-than-life photos of her jewelry. Accordingly, viewers often got a much better view of the top of her head than her face!

I worked with Melissa to help her become calmer and more present. She really needed to deal with the reality of her on-TV selling business, and the fact that people tuning in were sincerely interested in her work. This included, of course, the possibility of a continuing working relationship with that audience and additional audiences who had heard about her products. In other words, it definitely wasn't a one-time thing, with a single customer purchasing a product on display at the moment. Among other things, Melissa needed to be building a *brand*. (I'll have more to say on building your own brand in Chapter 13.)

In my sessions with Melissa, I focused considerably on breathing, especially diaphragmatic breathing. She had a tendency to take nervous shallow breaths, which not only worked against her feeling present and in control of the moment, but was probably noticeable to viewers.

What we discovered was that Melissa couldn't feel comfortable presenting her designs precisely because *her rapid breathing didn't allow her to feel physically at ease.* I also spent time on getting her to speak more slowly—not only to make the conversations more comfortable for prospective buyers who were watching, but also so that she herself would feel more relaxed. I knew that slowing and deepening her breathing was the key first step. By "re-learning" to breathe naturally, she could go from what felt like inner chaos, to a quieter interior space where she could feel more like herself.

It worked.

CHAPTER 2

'To Know Life In Every Breath': Breathing Techniques

Exercise 5: Testing Your Respiration Cycle

One surefire way to get a sense of how you're dealing with the environment around you is to test your respiration cycle. This is a term that simply means the number of inhalations and exhalations you typically go through in 60 seconds.

The idea of the test is for you to breathe normally (without thinking about it), then count the number of times you inhale and exhale in one minute. So:

Total inhalations + total exhalations in 60 seconds = Your score. That's it.

Here are the simple instructions:

DETERMINING YOUR RESPIRATION CYCLE

1. Set a timer or your smart phone to 1 minute.

2. Without trying to go slowly or rapidly or anything else, breathe in normally, then breathe out normally. It's just a typical day and you're, well, breathing without thinking about it, just as you do day in and day out. After you've inhaled and then exhaled for the first time, silently count, "One."

3. Inhale and exhale again, silently counting "Two."

4. Once more: a normal inhalation + a normal exhalation equals "Three," and so on.

5. Continue until the one minute is up and you have an overall count.

This is your respiration cycle, or the number of times you complete the action of breathing in one minute: 12, 20, 31, or whatever the number comes out to be. Now I'll tell you what the ideal is, and this number may shock you. It's 5.

When I first learned about the respiration cycle test some years ago and tried it myself, my result was...5. It's not unusual, however, for my clients to get a score in the teens, twenties, or even low thirties.

Here's the important thing to remember about your own number: it's a worthwhile indicator of how activated—or over-activated—you are by the environment around you. In other words, it's one measurement that shows your *response* to your surroundings and situation, i.e., your internal state as you're reacting to those stimuli. Another way to say this may make this idea clearer: a high respiration cycle is one of the symptoms of PTSD. Along with heart rate variability, the respiratory system's actions via the autonomic nervous system are negatively affected by psychological stress.[1]

In other words, too-rapid breathing is a reliable indicator that you're stressed or anxious. So, the respiration cycle test becomes a quick and easy way to judge how you're responding to your environment. Your nervous system is indicating—in a way that is easily measurable—when you may benefit from reducing how rapidly you're breathing.

The good news is that you can learn to slow down your respiration cycle through focus and simple biofeedback. (More on this a little later in this chapter.) For now, test your own cycle as explained above, and tuck that number into the back of your mind.

A TRUE STORY: "COME ON...YOU MEDITATE, RIGHT?"

Here's a true story about just how effective healthy breathing techniques can be in helping you deal with stress. For a number of years, I coached the keynote speakers at an annual healthcare conference that took place in Boston. At any large-scale regional or national meeting, of course, there are also exhibitors' booths, usually located in the middle of the venue's layout, where vendors market their products and make deals with the users of those products.

This particular year, one of the vendors in the exhibitors' section was the manufacturer of a headband that was meant to be used for stress-reduction. The instrument purportedly taps into electrical impulses in the brain which can then—through biofeedback practiced by the wearer—teach that person how to reduce mental stress. As I strolled by the booth, the salesperson, like a carnival barker, invited me to give the instrument a whirl. The test works like this: the subject (me in this case), puts on the headband, which includes headphones. I was told I had a choice of listening either to ocean waves or storm activity. I choose the stormy weather.

Then, for two or three minutes, you listen. In my case, I would be hearing thunder somewhat in the distance. The idea was that I was supposed to concentrate on *reducing* the level of storm activity, that is, to make the thunder softer and to keep it in the distance. If I was able to create a positive biofeedback loop, that's exactly what I'd hear: the sounds of thunder either remaining at the same volume level or getting more distant. If I *wasn't* successful in my attempt at generating helpful biofeedback, the storm would sound like it was getting closer and be that much louder.

I have to admit that not much seemed to be happening with my storm: the rumbles remained soft and distant. So, I decided to make things more interesting by trying to make my thoughts stressful and chaotic. I must have been thinking, "Let's get this party going!" But it was no good...my storm remained a wimpy one.

At the end of the time period, the salesperson told me my "score." It was 93. I had no idea if that was good or abysmal, but he said: "Nobody gets 93 on the first try. We had one of the Dalai Lama's assistants try the product—he teaches meditation, by the way—and his score was 95. You meditate, right?"

"Actually, no, I don't."

"Come *on*...you meditate, right?"

"No, really," I replied. "But I do coach and train people in dealing with fear and anxiety. And as a stage actor (and runner), I've spent years developing my breath capacity, and mindful calm breathing is an important part of my practice. It must have been my breathing that created the positive feedback loop and quieted the storm."

I believe that was literally true in the demonstration that day. And I'm convinced that by achieving your own slower and more controlled respiration cycle, you will be less likely to get drenched by your own mental storms.

One final thought: Thinking that the sales guy might have inflated my score to make me think the product was fantastic and I should order one right away, I sought out a colleague at the conference that I knew attended it every year. If he'd gone through with the same demonstration, I could realistically compare our scores.

"Did you ever do the _____ headband test?" I asked him.

"Yeah, last year."

"Do you remember what your score was?"

"Not exactly. Somewhere in the 40s."

Do you happen to know where I can contact the Dalai Lama's team for a job interview?

Exercise 6:
How to Breathe Naturally Again

Let's talk about diaphragmatic (pronounced "di-a-fra-MATIC") breathing. You've probably heard the term. The reason it's called this is because of the essential action of the *diaphragm*, a sheet of muscle between your chest cavity and abdomen that is essential for breathing to take place.

Simply put: there is no more important skill for you to master than to access your breathing mechanism in the most productive way. That's because it's hard-wired to your nervous system and helps to make you more aware, centered, and in touch with the moment.

Now, here's the really good news: you are already practicing diaphragmatic breathing. It's really just a question of *reintroducing* yourself to the best practices regarding this powerful tool of awareness and confidence.

The more you can maximize breathing via the full use of your diaphragm, the more natural your respiration will be. Babies and toddlers breathe this way because, again, it's completely natural. We often develop bad habits as we get older, however; and many times we end up breathing more shallowly than we should be doing. It's not hard to figure out why this is unhealthy: shallow breathing means less oxygen for all the cells of your body!

Here's how "natural" breathing works:

When you inhale, your diaphragm moves downward and flattens, creating room above it for the vertically expanding lungs. As the diaphragm descends, it pushes down on the abdominal area below it. Since the interior of the body has no spare real estate, your abdomen or "belly" has to go somewhere—which is outward. That's why your abdominal wall moves outward when you inhale, i.e., your belly protrudes, just like a balloon inflating.

When you exhale, on the other hand, your lungs grow smaller as they release air. Your diaphragm, no longer needing to be out of the way of the expanding lungs, can rise again and assume its relaxed "dome" shape. As a result, your belly (your abdominal area), which isn't being pushed out of the way by the diaphragm anymore moves back inward, returning to *its* former relaxed position.

To put all that together in terms of the simple movement you notice: your belly moves outward when you inhale and inward when you exhale. The classic example of this diaphragmatic action is a baby lying on its back in a crib: the baby's belly rises and falls noticeably with each inhalation-exhalation cycle.

PRACTICING DIAPHRAGMATIC BREATHING

Now it's your turn to practice this essential action of proper breathing. What's worth remembering is that you want the action of the diaphragm to be as full as possible. (None of the shallow breathing that's such a bad habit in our culture!)

The more the diaphragm can descend and get out of the way of the lungs, the more air the lungs will be able to take in. There are all kinds of advantages to having "a full reservoir" of air like this, from providing oxygen to all the cells of the body, to the creation of a pleasant and authoritative voice, to reducing your anxiety and avoiding the "fight or flight syndrome." In other words, breathing the right way will give you maximum oxygenation while contributing to your sense of confidence and well-being.

Here's how to do it.

- To begin, stand with good posture yet without tightening your torso anywhere. To breathe diaphragmatically, focus your attention on your abdominal area. This is where all of the action that you can observe should take place.

- Stand easily, without tension. Place your dominant hand on your belly, i.e., at the place that goes in and out most noticeably when you inhale. What you will be seeing and feeling is the action of the diaphragm causing your belly to move in and out. This is necessary because you can't feel or see the actual movement of the diaphragm inside you. *The more noticeable the movement of your belly as it moves in and out, the more you know that your diaphragm is working fully.*

- Take relaxed, deep breaths. On the inhalation, your belly should "inflate" under your hand; on the exhalation, it should return to its former position. This movement should be easy and effortless and, as I say above, quite noticeable.

- Be sure you are not "helping" your hand. Don't *do* anything; just breathe. Your hand will follow the natural movement of the abdominal wall that it is resting upon.

- Not noticing a huge amount of movement in your belly? There's no cause to be concerned. If you're "new" to diaphragmatic breathing (meaning if you've developed more shallow breathing habits over the years), the action may not be too noticeable at first. The more you practice, however, the better at it you will become.

- If you find that you're breathing "backwards"—sucking in your belly when you inhale and pushing it out when you exhale—be patient. This is not uncommon. Simply observe what's happening, and begin a new habit of getting the movement going in the right direction.

- MIRROR, MIRROR, ON THE WALL: If you stand in front of a mirror, you'll be able to see the movement more clearly. Stand at an angle that allows you to see your belly slightly in profile. Another helpful technique is to lie in a bathtub filled with warm water. You'll immediately notice that each time you inhale, you rise upward in the water, just like an inner tube being inflated; and when you exhale, you'll sink back down. What an enjoyable excuse to take a relaxing bath!

Belly breathing not only gives you a dependable supply of oxygen at all times. It's also a reliable tool for keeping you calmer and more in control in a stressful situation, when you need it most. Nothing will give you less of a sense of control, on the other hand, than feeling that your breathing is out of whack, which can lead to a whole cascade of negative body sensations.

The Picture of Confidence. There's also this benefit: when you stand straight with your breathing apparatus in alignment without slouching, you'll *look* like the picture of confidence. Try it now while you're in the vicinity of that mirror. First, let all of your breath out. Notice how you immediately take on a slightly caved-in appearance? Now, assume good posture while taking a deep diaphragmatic breath.

My, oh my! What a confident and capable-looking person you are!

Exercise 7: Are You Breathing Incorrectly? — 3 Ways to Tell

Now that you know how to breathe diaphragmatically, you can take the next step. That involves using your breath as a key tool to reduce anxiety, let go of your fears, and gain greater confidence when dealing with others. It all has to do with learning how to *control* the breath.

To start, I'll explain a little more about the natural way of breathing versus the bad habits I hinted at above. The reason is that you'll need to check that you're breathing correctly. Then I'll discuss the importance of *using your breath for more effective communication*. That's a unique application of the breath that you probably won't be exposed to except through a performance-based approach like the one offered in this book.

Incorrect Breathing #1: Active vs. Passive Breathing. The type of breathing you use in daily living is called *passive or vegetative breathing*. As that label indicates, this type of breathing doesn't take much effort. Talking to a colleague at the desk next to yours or at the coffee machine, or projecting your voice two inches into the phone aren't activities that demand much from your breathing mechanism.

Breathing capacity is an issue that still matters, however. When your respiration cycle is almost entirely passive, you're apt to breathe shallowly, taking in only a small amount of air. But speech requires your escaping breath to both activate your vocal folds and project your voice outward to one person or many. That requires *active*, not passive breathing. For one thing, a pleasant voice requires a cushion of air, not just the bare minimum to make yourself heard. To improve your vocal quality, then, start by breathing more deeply. Allowing yourself a full reservoir of air with each breath will give your voice more resonance, warmth, and carrying power.

Incorrect Breathing #2: Where the Action Takes Place. Obviously, to breathe this way is to use your breathing mechanism correctly. If that sounds like you have to learn something new and complicated, just the opposite is true: it simply means getting back to using your anatomy for breathing in a way that's so easy even a new-born baby does it without being conscious of it.

There are basically three ways to use the breathing mechanism, and only one of them is the correct method. You've already (re)learned the right one: DIAPHRAGMATIC BREATHING— the one that involves your belly expanding and contracting. If, on the other hand, you raise your shoulders each time you inhale, that's called CLAVICULAR BREATHING (named after your clavicle or collarbone). Or, if instead you raise your chest each time you inhale (you'll see it clearly when you do the mirror exercise), that's called THORACIC BREATHING because you're over-expanding your thorax. Both clavicular breathing and thoracic breathing are simply examples of wasted energy. Remember: all the action you want to be aware of should be taking place in your mid-section, as your diaphragm descends (so your lungs can fill), and as it descends, pushes your belly out.

Incorrect Breathing #3: Not Controlling the Respiration Cycle. Your *control* of the breathing cycle is where you can make it all come together to be in charge of your speech. To be fair, not doing this really doesn't qualify as "incorrect" breathing. Instead, you'll be throwing away a golden opportunity to be a more dynamic communicator. And why would you want that to happen?

It has to do with our language. Did you know that in English, the most important word usually comes at the end of an utterance? (I don't say "sentence," because we write in sentences, but we speak in ideas and emotions.)

For instance, probably the most famous spoken passage in

English is "To be or not to be, that is the *question*." Shakespeare didn't use some other arrangement that buries the central question of whether Hamlet should do away with himself—he placed it at the very end.

He *might* have said, for instance: "The question, really, is whether or not I should be or not be."

Yuck.

The whole point for the character is the painful human *question* he's dealing with, i.e., the decision he has to make, and so the word (and idea) comes at the very end.

All Breathing Is Not Equal. When you breathe passively, your inhalation and exhalation are about equal, i.e., they have the same duration. When you speak, however, the situation is entirely different. Remember, as stated above, that exhaled air is the source of the produced voice. *So every time you express an idea, you're likely doing it on one breath.* Of course, I realize that some ideas take many sentences, when they are written out, to be expressed, but I think you know what I'm getting at here: Each time you speak, you are controlling your exhalation, since it is tied to the outward expression of your idea.

For instance, if someone asks, "What's the weather like outside?" you most likely *automatically and unthinkingly* will take a short breath before you answer, "Cloudy and cool."

But it someone asks you, "What do you think of the ongoing unrest in the Middle East regarding Israel and Gaza? Do you think there's a solution everyone can agree on?" If that's the question, you're sure to take a deep breath before you begin to share your considered opinion!

In cases where you're really trying to share something of value in terms of what you're saying—in other words, the times when you're not just stating that the weather outside is cloudy—you need to *punch* the idea that comes at the end of your idea with adequate support and vocal energy (through the breath!) Why? Because we already know that the heart of what you *really mean* is coming at the end.

Some examples:

- JFK: "Ask not what your country can do for you…ask *what you can do for your country.*"

- Ronald Reagan: "General Secretary Gorbachev, if you seek peace, if you seek prosperity for the Soviet Union and Eastern Europe, if you seek liberalization: Come here to this gate! Mr. Gorbachev, open this gate! *Mr. Gorbachev, tear down this wall!*

And in our everyday world of personal and professional communication:

- "Son, I know you were angry with your sister…but *you musn't use your hands.*"

- "Oh, I didn't mean to step in front of you in line…*I'm very sorry.*"

- "Here at Perfect Manufacturers, we don't want to just sell products…we want to be *the world leader in our industry.*

If you're like some of my coaching clients who ask concerning an upcoming participation in a video meeting or presentation: "When should I become aware of diaphragmatic action to control my breathing?" my answer to you as well is simple:

"Always."

Breathing for speech, that is, should be a full-time pursuit for you. Of course, once you develop the habit of full diaphragmatic breathing, it won't need to be a conscious activity at all, even when you're about to say something important. You'll take the breath(s) you need without thinking about it, because it's getting the idea across that will be uppermost in your mind, not how you're breathing!

At the same time, there are other breathing techniques that function as powerful tools to reduce your stress response, help quiet your fears, and keep you in the moment so you can think on your feet and respond to the situation at hand—even at the most stressful of times.

Keep reading to find out what they are!

Exercise 8: The Amazing Power of Exhalation

Here's another great reason to practice mindful breathing: Controlled breathing can help reduce any tension and tightness you feel *physically* in situations that stress you or make you anxious.

Although you may not always be aware of it, there is a direct connection between your thinking and emotions (especially your emotions) and how your body responds. So, the truth is, you can't just *think* your way out of stressful situations. It helps tremendously if you can get your body into the act, so that you feel in control of your physical response. You already know that if your mind and emotions are in turmoil, you're not going to be mentally in control of your reactions. Well, the same is true of your body!

Here, then, is a simple yet highly efficient exercise that allows you to channel the inner control you're trying to achieve directly into physical relaxation. Achieving such "agreement" of mind and body is a highly positive synergy. This exercise is called "The Directed Breath." Here's how it's done:

- You should practice this exercise while sitting or standing, because it's most helpful if done just before you make an appearance. Start out with the slow, controlled belly breathing you've already learned in this chapter. Again, you'll eventually be aiming for 5 or 6 respiration cycles per minute (remember, one inhalation + one exhalation = 1 respiration cycle). But don't worry about holding yourself to that slow rate of breathing at this point. If it feels unnatural at this stage or you feel oxygen deprived, go ahead and breathe at a rate that works for you.

- Once you're breathing relatively slowly and deeply, scan your body for any signs of tightness or tension. Are your shoulders hunched up? Is there a knot at the back of your neck? Do you feel tightness in your lower back? Are your jaws slightly clenched?, etc.

- Now, take a deep breath, and *direct your exhaled breath to that spot with a giant WHOOSH!* That is, imagine that you're exhaling fully *into* that tense place in your body. If you're tight in more than one place, concentrate on each location in turn. Obviously, you can't actually exhale through your shoulders or lower back. This is simply a visualization technique that makes your body an active partner in relaxing you physically.

Did it work? You may find that on the very first exhalation, you feel some release of the tension at that place in your body. And of course, it's certainly worth knowing that your breath alone can help untie your muscular tension.

Here's another important way this visualization can help you if you're feeling anxious or stressed when dealing with others. Whenever we interact with people, whether it's in conversations or public settings, we help ourselves tremendously when we can stay flexible and able to adapt to the situation.

Many of the exercises in this book help you do that mentally and emotionally. The Directed Breath adds a physical dimension to literally relax you in terms of your musculature. It can help you feel freer and more flexible (rather than tense), and therefore more able to go with the flow physically as well as mentally!

Exercise 9: Inspiration for Conquering Fear

in.spi.ra.tion
1. a breathing in, as of air into the lungs; inhaling. 2. an inspiring or being inspired mentally or emotionally. 3. an inspiring influence; any stimulus to creative thought or action (*Webster's New World Dictionary, Second College Edition*).

Surprised to hear that the first dictionary definition of "inspiration" has to do with *breathing*? Yet that's completely appropriate, since clear thinking as well as being relaxed and calm both begin with getting oxygen where it's needed.

Among the benefits of learning how to be "inspired" in this way is using the breath to reduce anxiety.

Calming the Storm. If you struggle with being relaxed and fully present in professional situations, the first order of business is quieting down the noise and inner chaos interfering with your comfort level and focus. Good breathing is not only ideal for getting you calm and concentrated—it's one of the few ways that you *can* reach that state.

Let's face it: the loss of control you suffer can make it seem as though an electrical storm were taking place inside you! The secret is to enter the *eye of the storm*, where things are calm and quiet. From this peaceful center, you can heal, rejuvenating yourself and "turn down the volume" as you begin to apply appropriate coping mechanisms.

The Willow Tree Visualization. Here's a visualization that may help make this clearer: Imagine a willow tree in the middle of a thunderstorm. High winds are torturing the slender branches of that tree, thrashing them violently, and the willow's wisp-like leaves make the movement all the more dramatic. That's what it can feel like when you lose control or find yourself at the mercy of negative outside influences. But now, visualize the *trunk* of the willow tree during the same storm: it's unmoving, stable, unaffected by anything except true hurricane-force winds.

Using Breath to Conquer Fear. As the first step in using breath to conquer fear, I'd like you to imagine that your breath emanates from your core, just like that tree trunk in the storm. Rather than the thrashing branches, your breathing is as steadfast and unwavering as the trunk of the willow tree—your breath itself is the source of your calmness and stability.

So whenever things seem to be getting just a little out of control, remember that *your breathing is your center. You must always come back to the BREATH, for that is where life itself and peacefulness exist.*

Get to that place, and you'll be far more in control of whatever is happening around you and your personal response to it. It's a reliable starting point for getting to the eye of the storm, where you can let go, rejuvenate, and *think*.

Exercise 10: Breathing and the Present Moment

I believe that the need to be in the present moment is nowhere—or no *time*—more pressing than it is right now in the 21st century.

In the past, changes to the way people lived their lives often took centuries to evolve. If your parents were farmers and you worked on the farm as a child, you would most likely take over that farm when it was time to do so. If your father was a master mason, you would probably be one too. If your mother had other children and was a homemaker, that's the role you would be expected to fill when you grew up.

Yet nowadays, you may find yourself eager to add the latest app to the impossibly long list of those you're already checking in with on a daily basis. Yet despite our more frantic lives, our need for a mindful response to the world around us is the same as it's always been.

But that need clashes with one of the biggest challenges we face today: our sense that time is becoming increasingly warped. How can we "relax" into a life and live it if that life constantly seems to be morphing into something else at light speed? Our enslavement to the digital world…the mind-jarring shifts in our attention that occur from constant multitasking…ever-multiplying social media channels clamoring for our attention… the never-ending assault on our focus (and our wallets) from the advertisers and marketers that hound us everywhere we go and on every screen within our view; add our shrinking attention spans due to TV shows, commercials, and movies that substitute speed and frantic action for meaning—all of these phenomena, in their own way, change how we experience life and how slowly or quickly we sense the passing of time *and what we expect from it*. (Did you, in fact, become impatient with that last intentionally complex sentence?)

These continual demands on our brain and nervous system lead to what Dennis Lewis, author of *Free Your Breath, Free Your Life* describes as "a low-grade but chronic fight or flight or freeze state, in which…the constant release of adrenaline and cortisol undermines our immune system and throws us into increasingly negative states of disharmony."[2]

Are You Wrapped Up In the Speed Of It All? The danger, of course, is that this stressed-out state becomes your norm— that you consider it a *necessary* response to your environment. Then, it seems, you're reduced to just two speeds in your personal response-a-meter: stop and fast-forward.

But although society and the present state of science and technology seem to be determined to hurl ahead at warp speed, your body can't follow. Just one hundred and fifty years ago, the telephone hadn't yet been invented! (It arrived the following year.) That may seem like ancient history today, but it takes *millions* of years for physical changes and adaptations of our species to take place.

Stability and Timelessness Come from the Present Moment. So, here's a way to appreciate the present moment and give yourself some stability and a sense of timelessness that will bring your mind, body, and soul into synch. It starts and ends with the realization that *there is nothing that makes up your life except* *present moments.* Whatever happened in the past is in the rear-view mirror, and there *is* no mirror that will allow you to see what is coming. And so you can't live in either of those dimensions.

Every *real* moment of your life is what you're experiencing right here and now—in this very second. To be aware of that, to be *mindful* of living in the present moment, is to actually experience your life!

Remember, it is breathing that more than anything brings you back to the moment at hand, *your* moment in life. So use this always-available, easy tool to return to where you want and need to be: present, centered, and at ease in your world. Don't let your mind hijack your life.

Breathe, and come back to the present.

NOTES

1 "Autonomic dysfunction in posttraumatic stress disorder indexed by heart rate variability: a meta-analysis." Published online by Cambridge University Press: 28 August 2020. https://www.cambridge.org/core/journals/psychological-medicine/article/autonomic-dysfunction-in-posttraumatic-stress-disorder-indexed-by-heart-rate-variability-a-metaanalysis/777778EA3BEEDC3DF66A9F24F975F4DB

2 Dennis Lewis. *Free Your Breath, Free Your Life* (Boston: Shambhala, 2004), 98.

CHAPTER 3

The Neurology of Fear and Anxiety

Exercise 11: The Limbic System

In this chapter, you'll learn about the physical systems that underlie your fearful and anxious responses. For most of the chapter, that means systems in the brain. Except for the last exercise, you won't be doing things as much as you will be learning about the parts of your brain that create challenges for you in overcoming fear and anxiety. These structures—principally the limbic system and the amygdala—are essential to survival and well-being, and there are important reasons they were part of our evolution as a species. The more you know about them, the more you'll benefit from the knowledge, and will then be able to put together constructive responses to situations that typically make you fearful or anxious.

THE BRAIN AND EMOTIONS

The Prefrontal Cortex and Limbic System

Homo sapiens, means 'wise' or thinking human being. That attribute—so critical to your nature as a member of the dominant species—can get in your way when it comes to dealing with your emotional reactions to stressful situations. That's because it can be hard to turn your powerful thinking brain off!

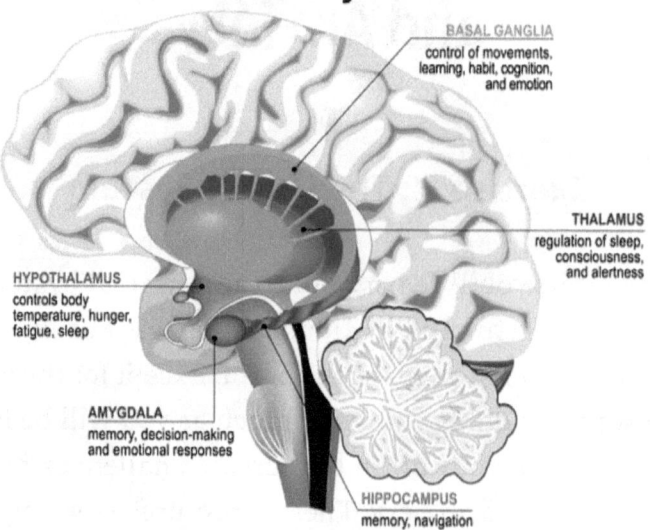

Illustration credit: designua, 123RF

The executive part of your brain, the *prefrontal cortex*, is designed to control thought, reasoning, emotion, and planning. And in the human brain, it's really massive. The prefrontal cortex takes up nearly one-third of the neocortex or outer layer of the brain. In our nearest relatives the chimpanzee, the prefrontal cortex is only 17% of the neocortex. In a dog, it's 13%, and only 4% in a cat.[1]

An important part of the prefrontal cortex is the *limbic system*, a C-shaped structure deep in the brain, which is that organ's emotional center. While generating emotional responses, the limbic system also communicates with the centers of higher consciousness, and is involved in instinctive behaviors.[2]

Limbic 'Memory' and Learned Behavior

Another function of the limbic system that's important for you to know is *its power to embed emotional memories*. Pleasant, dangerous, or otherwise significant events you experience in your life are encoded via the limbic system as encounters you remember—long after the original encoding event. This has particular significance regarding 'learned events' or 'learned behavior'. These are negative experiences (often but not always occurring when you were young) in which you 'learn' that something is dangerous, unpleasant, frightening, or just an activity that you don't do well. Significantly for our purposes in this book, learned behavior can undermine your confidence or even your sense of well-being for years after the original event or situation.

Here's an actual example of learned behavior. We'll call this person Graciela. When Graciela was a young girl, her sister locked her in a closet and left the room for some minutes. It was a terrifying experience because it taught Graciela how vulnerable she was.

She added hastily after telling me this: "I love my sister dearly, and we're great friends as adults." Yet that event of long ago undermined her confidence in *any* situation where she feels vulnerable. Notice how in this instance, the initiating event had nothing to do with any kind of performance or competence. It didn't matter—her limbic brain retained this traumatic emotional memory under a category of 'Situations where I'm vulnerable and should be afraid.' Her learned, fearful thinking and behavior now comes to life when she's under pressure or in the spotlight and therefore feels exposed and fearful.

Let's look more closely at the section of the brain which actually sets off the alarm bells. This is the area that's involved when fear rears its head, or you start to feel panicky. It's called the *amygdala*, and it too is squarely at the intersection of something happening in your life that elicits a fearful response from you.

Exercise 12: The Amygdala

The amygdala is a small, almond-shaped structure in the limbic system whose task is to sort through emotions. (You can see its location in the drawing of the limbic system, above.)

The job of the amygdala is to gather emotional stimuli and determine their significance, including whether a threat is present. It is worth noting, however, that the amygdala's activity doesn't only result in fearful reactions. In its function to get a 'rapid response' going as fast as possible, it doesn't spend time examining the overall situation. It wants to get you to *remember your emotional response to interesting phenomena*, including whether any particular phenomenon is dangerous or merely interesting to you.

Of course, once you become afraid of something, you are programmed to recall that stimulus in strongly negative terms, and so from that point on are conditioned *toward* that fear.[3] That's why you may become agitated in recurring situations that are similar to the original event or stimulus.

So even though like all human beings you've evolved a highly sophisticated thinking and processing brain (the prefrontal cortex), you're still at the mercy of primitive emotions derived from the amygdala any time you sense danger. (And keep in mind, the danger doesn't have to be real, as long as you *perceive* it to be real.) In other words, you respond quickly and powerfully to what your emotional brain is telling you. Daniel Goleman, the popularizer of emotional intelligence, writes about the direct link between the amygdala and the human fear response:

> The amygdala is central to fear. When a rare brain disease destroyed the amygdala (but no other brain structures) in the patient neurologists call "S.M.," fear disappeared from her mental repertoire. She became unable to identify looks of fear on other people's faces, nor to make such an expression herself. As her neurologist put it, "If someone put a gun to S.M.'s head, she would know intellectually to be afraid but she would not feel afraid as you or I would."[4]

Such a powerful stimulus *telling you to be afraid* at appropriate moments can literally be lifesaving. However, it can become a problematic response in scenarios where you're not actually in a threatening situation. In those cases, the amygdala's warning signal becomes an *inappropriate reaction*, yet one that at the same time can be difficult to overcome. What happens is that you're caught in the dilemma of your brain screaming "Danger!" when the situation isn't a threat to your survival at all (such as, for instance, "important" meetings and appearances where you know you have to be at your best).

But the brain doesn't care. As far as it's concerned, this is the moment to activate your physical mechanism to get you out of that danger as fast as possible. This is the well-known "fight-or-flight response." Because your survival is at stake (or so your amygdala perceives), this physiological response takes place at lightning speed—before, in fact, you have any time to think about it.

That is, the amygdala is so good at processing emotional stimuli that it does its thing before you even sense what is happening! The reason is to allow your body to react instantaneously, without thought. Once your body has done so and kicked into high gear and begun taking some action, the frontal cortex comes back online, starting to sort through the information you're receiving in a more rational process.[5]

"Ah," your brain *now* says, "This isn't really a life-threatening situation at all. It's only _____. Okay everybody, stand down."

By this time, however, it's too late to turn off the overwhelming physiological reaction you're going through. Stress hormones including epinephrine (adrenalin), cortisol, and norepinephrine have already flooded into your bloodstream. These are powerful chemicals produced by the adrenal gland that prime you for *action*. Other changes occur. Your pupils dilate; your blood is redistributed to the large muscles you need to fight or flee; and digestion and peristalsis (the forward movement of waste products through the intestines) cease...because you don't have the luxury of dealing with them at the moment.

All of these coordinated responses are wonderfully efficient in terms of getting you to survive life-threatening situations. However, if you experience them chronically —through constant feelings of anxiety at work, for instance—they become physically harmful by causing tissue damage and other undesirable effects within the body.

So here's where you are at this point: Your prefrontal cortex is trying to rationally sort out what is happening and whether you should be concerned. But the amygdala's alarm has gone off, sending out signals to every major area of the brain. These signals impact the cardiovascular system, muscles, eyes, gut, diaphragm, and lungs—all systems you need to make you alert and physically responsive to the 'threat'. And the entire process—perception of danger, physiological super-activation, and the thinking brain's attempt to figure out what's actually happening—takes all of about a second.

Negative Cognitive Bias

In addition to your rapid (and powerful) emotional and physical responses, you may also be dealing with some negative cognitive bias. This refers to the tendency to zero in on possibly negative or dangerous outcomes while excluding potentially rewarding ones.

As you can gather from the explanation above, your brain is capable of focusing at the speed of milliseconds—too fast for you even to be conscious that it's happening—on whatever part of the environment seems important to you. If you are cognitively biased toward negative outcomes—that is, if you're constantly looking out for them, you'll be getting an inaccurate picture of the world. In effect, you will see things as hazardous, even dangerous, not because they are so, but because you are expecting them to be that way.[6] It's easy to imagine, isn't it, how this can *constantly* and reliably undermine your confidence in certain recurring situations?

There's even a way to measure negative cognitive bias. A recent experiment, for example, found that people with social anxiety pay more attention to what they consider negative faces than positive ones.[7] They are at the mercy of their bias. For instance, they may imagine that most (or all) of the people at a gathering are unfriendly toward them simply because they're fixated on a few unwelcoming faces!

Exercise 13: Is It All In Your Mind?

Well, yes, of course it is.

And no, it isn't.

If you're extremely apprehensive about a situation you're in or about to enter, in addition to your fear you may feel confused. As an example: you may know quite well that you're an expert in your field, with years of experience and no problems discussing your work. So, you may wonder why in the world you have such difficultly introducing yourself in virtual or in-person meetings to people you don't know.

Somewhere along the line, you may have heard about the Imposter Syndrome, and think:

"Yes, that's it! That's what I'm going through."

What we call Imposter Syndrome exists across all ages, sexes, and ethnic groups. Encyclopaedia Britannica defines it this way:

> A persistent unjustified feeling that one's success is fraudulent. Imposter syndrome is characterized by doubt in one's abilities—despite a record of achievement or respect from one's peers—and a fear of having one's unworthiness exposed. Imposter syndrome was first described in 1978 by researchers at Georgia State University on the basis of observations of high-achieving women undergoing psychotherapy.[8]

So you see, this condition has been recognized for nearly 50 years. But you can also be certain that it's existed for much longer than that, whether it had a psychological label or not.

When you're in the grip of fears, lack of confidence, nagging worries, along with thoughts that you're not good enough—or even overall confusion about why you feel this way—you probably do what any rational person would do. You try to reason out the causes, examples, and ramifications of your perceived inabilities, so you can then do something to remedy them.

But fear isn't a rational process. It's a deeply imbedded *emotional* response—one of the most primitive and powerful reactions you experience. Fear has saved the lives of some of your ancestors. And it's just as valuable to you today. Courage, for instance, doesn't exist in the absence of fear. In fact, it's just the opposite. What makes a person do something brave isn't a matter of disregarding the danger with a wave of their hand and charging into the fray. Bravery is being frightened out of your mind and doing what you think you must do anyway.

It also doesn't do any good to tell yourself that your particular fearful or anxious response is all in your mind without any real substance. It's true, as we've seen above, that there are powerful neurological reactions that are responsible for your fear. Yet you experience the feelings you do because of triggers in the real world, and you make choices and often perform physical actions as a result.

British voice coach Patsy Rodenburg, who works with high-profile actors on the English stage, claims that according to a medical study: "An actor going onstage for a press night—when theater critics and the press are invited—undergoes the same tension as a victim in a major car accident."[9]

That certainly indicates major stress. Just like you, the actor is going through the enormous challenge of realizing that he or she will be judged on their *performance.* But that certainly isn't a word that's confined to dramatic performance! We all must perform up to the expectations of our job, our colleagues, our boss, and of course, the people we interact with. And we also want to "perform" well as a husband or wife, father or mother, son or daughter, aunt or uncle or grandparent, friend, confidant to our closest friends, and as a person of morality, goodwill, kindness, and so on.

Whatever apprehensions or anxieties you're dealing with, you didn't spin them out of thin air. They grew out of what is happening to you *in the real world.* Yes, as we've seen, your brain has a key role in producing the emotional responses you're going through, via systems and anatomical structures that are critically important to your survival and awareness of the world around you.

But all of it certainly isn't *only* in your mind! That's what I want you to remember. The second thing is, being in a heightened state of anxiety—especially over a long period of time—risks your physical as well as your mental health. The next exercise explains why.

Exercise 14: The Dangers of Cortisol

Fear and anxiety not only result in psychological distress. They can also produce marked physiological responses. Such reactions can negatively affect how you feel physically. These constant reminders of negative body sensations can make it harder for you to let go of your fears i.e., it no longer is a question of just quieting the mind. Your body is now demanding relief as well.

When this happens, it's sometimes true that you show outwardly how you're feeling to others (think of reacting nervously, looking like you're on edge, sweating, breathing rapidly, trying to stop your hands from shaking if you're in front of an audience, etc.).

This tendency of your body to respond so strongly to anxiety, but especially fear, is the reason why any approach concerning how confident you feel and *appear* that focuses only on your mind isn't enough. You need to get your body into the act—and in a positive way!

Let's look first at the reasons your body reacts in ways that are clearly counter-productive to your sense of well-being and your displayed confidence. The following exercise covers the ways you can enlist your body's calming mechanisms instead. These work to counteract the "exciting" agents that can put you in a tailspin, since they use your own nervous system to place you in a resting and calm state.

THE EFFECTS OF CORTISOL

One of the most pronounced physical responses that occurs when you are fearful or anxious is the release of a stress hormone known as *cortisol*. Cortisol is a naturally occurring hormone produced by the adrenal glands.

Despite its reputation as an inducer of a stress-based hormonal response, cortisol has a positive role to play in your physiology. The beneficial effects of this substance include the following functions:

- Processing of glucose level in the body
- Regulating blood pressure
- Production of insulin to control blood sugar

- A healthy immune system
- Controlling inflammation

A problem arises, however, when there are prolonged high levels of stress-related cortisol in your bloodstream. A *chronic or frequent* state of anxiety or fearfulness—causing cortisol to continually flood the bloodstream—has been shown to have harmful effects on the body. These include:

- Decreased cognitive abilities
- Suppression of thyroid function
- High blood sugar
- Impairment of bone density
- Reduction in muscle tissue
- Increased blood pressure
- Reduced immune system function and response to inflammation
- Abdominal fat deposits, which are associated with health problems such as heart attack and strokes[110]

Clearly, you need a tool that will help you counter such a too-frequent stress response. Otherwise, your physical well-being is in danger of being compromised by your own nervous system's actions!

What is that tool? It's biofeedback. Let's take a look at how you can use it to *change your entire nervous system's response.*

Exercise 15: Activating the Vagus Nerve

BREATHING AND ANXIETY REDUCTION

In Chapter 2, you learned about natural breathing techniques that will help you to remain calm, centered, and "in the present moment." Don't forget: nervousness and fear can make you so focused on trying to survive what you consider a perilous situation that you can forget to breathe! You may have noticed speakers who exhibit this behavior, or perhaps it's happened to you while speaking.

This scenario can be turned on its head, however—for your breath is also a potent weapon for *reducing fear and anxiety*. It's all a question of gaining control of the breathing mechanism, while activating some powerful calming reactions of your nervous system.

THE SYMPATHETIC VS. PARASYMPATHETIC NERVOUS SYSTEMS

As I explained earlier, your physiological response to what appears to be a dangerous situation is instantaneous and overwhelming. When (you think that) your survival is at stake, your brain is willing to wait a while to understand what's really happening. The first and irresistible demand is the need to get you, i.e., your body, out of the hazardous situation as quickly as possible. And so the "fight or flight" response kicks in.

The amazing thing is that this happens in *less than one second* from when your brain senses danger! But that's long enough for your physical response to cascade into hyper mode—the pounding heart, rapid breathing, sweating, redistribution of your blood to your arms, hands, legs and feet (the better to fight or run with), dilation of your pupils so you can see the danger better—and any other physiological change that prepares you to actively resist or escape the situation at hand.

By the time this happens, it's too late to do anything about it—the stress hormones are now rushing through your bloodstream, and it will take some time for them to be reabsorbed by your body. Concerning our frenemy cortisol in particular, this process can take several hours.

What is happening in these situations is that your SYMPATHETIC NERVOUS SYSTEM goes into full operating mode. In a sense, it begins working overtime immediately, a from-zero-to-sixty scenario. In fact, the other name for this nervous system reaction is the well-known "fight or flight" response. Naturally, the physiological changes it forces on you via stress hormones are very much part of the discomfort or anxiety you feel.

Heading Off the Fight-or-Flight Response. But what if you could learn how to head off the sympathetic nervous system response before it can release its stress hormones? In other words, to get your body in the right mode before the anxiety-provoking situation shows up, so in effect you're armed and ready?

That's what I'm going to show you how to do right now. It involves using your breath to turn on *the other major response of your nervous system*. That's the one that will calm you down. And if you can turn it on prior to your spiking anxiety, it will protect you from being overactivated and overwhelmed.

It's called the PARASYMPATHETIC NERVOUS SYSTEM. It's nickname is "the rest-and-digest system"—a deliberate and rhyming counter-nickname to the "fight-or-flight system." And you can easily access it by breathing in one of two ways (or both ways), which I'll explain below. The idea is to enlist the para-sympathetic or "resting" response when you suspect an anxiety-provoking situation is on its way. In other words, you can call upon it at the moments when you need it most!

ENLISTING THE POWER OF THE VAGUS NERVE

What you're actually doing when you turn on the calming mode is activating the *vagus nerve*. This is the longest cranial nerve in the body (you actually have them on both sides), running all the way from your head to your abdomen. One of the important functions of the vagus nerve is that it regulates the heartbeat by speeding up the heart slightly upon inhalation and slowing it down upon exhalation.

That last part is worth repeating: *the vagus nerve slows down your heart rate every time you exhale.* Equally important, it's also responsible for switching on the parasympathetic nervous system. And again, it's the act of exhalation that makes this happen. So the answer to reigning in both your galloping heart and too-high respiration rate—the two most noticeable indicators of your heightened fear and anxiety—is really a simple one: *make your exhalation longer than your inhalation.*

The 4-4-6-2 Pattern. Breathing in this pattern automatically extends your exhalation so it's longer in duration than your inhalation. When you do this, you're basically instructing your vagus nerve to slow down your heart rate. The pattern is simple: you inhale for a silent count of four; pause for the same count; exhale for a silent count of six; then stop for a count of two. Then begin it all again, and continue in this way for at least two minutes.

Don't be surprised if you find this breathing pattern *very* relaxing. In fact, you should feel that way very quickly! (Avoid driving or operating machinery when you're doing this exercise, since it can even make you sleepy.) Also, feel free to adjust the duration of any of the numbers if you feel oxygen starved. If counting up to 6 is too long a time to exhale, make it 5, but then be sure to adjust the inhalation to 3 instead of 4. The idea is that your exhalation should be about 1 ½ times as long as your inhalation.

The Benefits of Physical Response. You've just learned about a very powerful tool to help you control the physiological effects of stress that can take control of you. Chapters 5, 6, and 7, on the other hand, will introduce you to mind-based approaches to reducing your anxiety and letting go of your fears.

Breathing to get the vagus nerve to turn on your parasympathetic nervous system, on the other hand, is entirely *physical*. By practicing this simple form of mindful breathing, you'll be giving yourself a powerful protective tool when anxiety is pressuring you to lose control.

NOTES

1   Rich Karlgaard, "It's Never Too Late to Start a Brilliant Career," *The Wall Street Journal*, May 4-5, 2019, C1.

2   Rita Carter. *The Human Brain Book (London: DK Publishing, 2014), 64.*

3   John Ratey. *A User's Guide to the* Brain (New York: Pantheon, 2001), 232.

4   Daniel Goleman, *Emotional Intelligence* (New York: Bantam, 1995), 297.

5   Carter, 126-127.

6   Caroline Williams, *My Plastic Brain* (Amherst, NY: Prometheus, 2018), 77-78.

7   Hofmann and Otto, *Cognitive Behavioral Therapy for Social Anxiety Disorder*, 16, citing a study by L.-G. Lundh and L.-G. Öst, "Recognition bias for critical faces in social phobics," in *Behaviour Research and Therapy, 34*, 787-794 (1996). In the study, subjects with social anxiety disorder or SAD and controls were asked to judge from photographs whether people were critical or accepting in nature. After performing an unrelated task, both groups were given a facial recognition test. People with social anxiety disorder more easily recognized the people they thought had critical faces, while the control subjects had a tendency to recall "accepting" faces. Quoted in Genard, *Fearless Speaking*, 96.

8   https:www.britannica.com/topic/imposter-syndrome

9   Quoted in Mel Gussow, "Henry Higgins Is Real (and Female)," *The New York Times*, January 8, 2001.

10 http://stress.about.com/od/stresshealth/a/cortisol.htm.

CHAPTER 4

Getting To Know Your Body

Exercise 16: The Physical You

Whether you turn heads at the beach or consider yourself a modest anatomical specimen, your body is one of your most important tools for confidently and comfortably occupying your world and dealing with others. Yet chances are you're not using this marvelous instrument—your body—as effectively as you can when you communicate with others. When you do, you'll not only feel all the benefits of a calm yet energetic state; you'll also broadcast relaxation, focus, and confidence.

You probably already know that *nonverbal communication* is a key element in all of this. It is vital to both your internal sensations and thoughts, and how accurately you interpret the way people respond to you. And, of course, it happens just as strongly in the opposite direction—in terms of how others make sense of *your* physical actions in terms of how you look, stand, move, gesture, and what you are telling them (and revealing to them) through your eye contact and facial expressions. This is truly "a language of the body," and people use it to make judgments about who you are and what your intentions are toward them.

Your Brand In Action. In fact, this nonverbal form of communication is going back and forth at a furious rate when humans interact. In terms of what *you* are sending out for others to react to, consider the following aspects of your persona that people determine from your nonverbal behavior. (Sometimes, that's *all* they are responding to!) Let's call it part of your "brand." All of these attributes are linked to what you show physically:

- Composure
- Intention
- Self-confidence
- Emotional stability
- Leadership abilities
- Self-control
- Experience
- Level of comfort and ease
- Power or powerlessness
- Directness of eye contact (or lack thereof)
- Balance
- Nervousness or calmness
- Muscular tension vs. relaxation
- Extroversion vs. introversion
- Trustworthiness
- Vigor
- Fitness
- Flexibility
- Friendliness
- Openness or lack thereof

- Command of the room or situation
- Fear or anxiety
- Contentment or well-being

Of course, this is not an exhaustive list. How important are these attributes concerning who other people think you are based on your body language? Remember this: *every one of the traits listed above that people assign to you can be determined solely from what you demonstrate physically!*

In other words, you're on display any time you're out in public. Moment by moment, the way you hold yourself and move and relate to other people is telling them who you are and what type of person you represent.

Are some of the conclusions people reach about you inaccurate? Of course! That's exactly why the more educated you become about what you're showing through your body language, the better you'll be able to display the "brand" you want the world to see.

CONSISTENCY vs. CHANGE

Let's look for a moment at how body language is portrayed in popular culture these days.

Books on body language and "experts" opining in interviews and podcasts on newsmakers' "tells" are especially popular. Because of that popularity, together they have increased awareness of the importance of nonverbal communication. At the same time, however, they've served up a huge heap of erroneous information in terms of the ways in which people actually interact and communicate with each other.

How? Well, for one thing, books, articles, and comments on

this topic tend to zero in on people's physical reactions, facial expressions, voice, etc., *in isolation*, and then tell us what it all means. The rules these experts share (they're always called "body language experts") tend to be rigid and simplistic, however, which is telling us right away that these commentators aren't really knowledgeable about body language at all.

For instance, have you learned any of the following "rules"?

- Crossed arms means resistance.
- A woman tucking her hair behind her ears is giving positive sexual signals.
- A glance by the speaker to his or her right while answering a question signals lying.

And so on.

The truth is, isolated physical responses like these mean little or nothing. Professionals whose job it is to rigorously read body language—customs officials, police interrogators, cross-examining attorneys, and so on—know that what really matters is *a change in a pattern of behavior.* In other words, when gestures, vocal qualities, or the rhythm of answers suddenly start to differ from what came previously, a red flag will pop up in the experienced interrogator's mind. That person then knows to probe a little more deeply into whatever was being discussed when the new pattern of behavior began to show itself. This probing via follow-up questions can then help determine whether there is a fire in sight, or just smoke.

Physical Expression Is More Than Just Gestures. Basically, one of the body's jobs when you're dealing with others is to *support* or *amplify* what you're saying by providing a visceral, visual expression of your ideas. In fact, rather than "body language," I use the term *physical expression* or *physical expressiveness*, because that in fact is what's going on. You are expressing what you are thinking and feeling physically along with the other ways you do so. Your stance, movement, and gestures function as powerful *amplifiers* of the things you're saying and thinking. They are, therefore, adding an important visual dimension that colors both the points you're making and your interactions with the people you're talking to through your willingness to engage them physically.

Naturally, the more comfortable you are with your physical self and the more you know about body language, the more likely you'll be putting out positive signals that accurately reflect your state of mind. The opposite, i.e., not being aware of the signals you're sending, can lead to weak or inappropriate physical expression that may be interpreted as being *opposed* to the way you really feel! When it comes to your physical expressiveness, people will naturally react to what you're showing rather than what you're thinking, since they can't read your thoughts.

BROADCASTING CONFIDENCE

Why do visuals matter so much when you're dealing with others?

To answer that, another question is necessary: Did you know that the average American spends *eight hours a day* in front of a screen of some kind: television, computer, cell phone, tablet, e-reader, and so on?[1] We have been relentlessly trained to be visual learners. Naturally, then, people will respond most strongly to the *visual* messages you're sending out in terms of how you look, stand, move, etc.

One of the problems you will run into, therefore, in social and professional settings if you don't understand your physical self well enough—if you don't "know your own body"—is that you may be sending out the *wrong* signals. And from those mismatched cues, people will make erroneous judgments and decisions about you that may not accurately reflect your thoughts, feelings, and intentions at all! Take the classic example of someone who has not broken any law, but appears extremely nervous when he or she walks by a police officer or sees a police cruiser coming down the street. The officers will automatically think, "Why is this person acting so jumpy? Are they guilty of something?"

The Solution? — Broadcasting Confidence. Now, what happens if the opposite occurs: if you "broadcast confidence" and use body language skillfully? Here are some positive outcomes that can occur if that is the case:

- You come across as a credible and confident person who seems to enjoy what you're doing.

- Your voice supports your message with sufficient power and resonance (vocal production is a physical, not a verbal process, so it's part of nonverbal communication).

- You seem more comfortable in your skin.

- Challenges and obstacles—and even resistance—don't intimidate you. (After all, you're showing your confidence through some of the ways mentioned above.)

- You appear to be accessible, i.e., not stiff and defensive but open to others. This automatically makes you more likable and therefore more persuasive.

That's not a bad set of advantages from simply "looking the part," is it?

WHAT IS YOUR BODY SAYING?
— THE IMPORTANCE OF POSTURE

One last point—this one about posture.

Though it may not seem like the most vital aspect of your physical self, posture is important in terms of exhibiting confidence and a sense of authority (including taking control and looking the part when you are in the spotlight).

Think of it this way: *How you stand affects your* standing *with your audience.*

Try this simple exercise:

Stand in front of a mirror. If your posture (your "standing!") needs to improve—if you slouch with shoulders hunched or lean backward putting too much pressure on your lower back—here's a visualization that can help:

> *Imagine there's a string leading upward from the top of your head into infinity.*

Someone up there is gently and steadily pulling on that string (not jerking it). This "pulls you up," and helps you to slowly straighten your posture. Gradually, your hips, waist, shoulders, neck, and head each "separate" from each other and fall into their natural alignment.

Your posture is now straight but not stiff.

Here's an alternate technique: Stand with your back against a wall, with your head, backside, and heels all touching the wall. Take a small step forward then relax slightly. Your posture is now improved, though again, not stiff or rigid.

The following exercise, titled "Grounding," is another visualization that can help improve your posture. But it really does something much more powerful as well: it brings you closer to a commanding physical presence. It's a fundamental tool of performance that comes to you straight from the world of the actor. In your case, the stage you perform on isn't in a theater—it's the world around you. "All the world's a stage," said Shakespeare, and he was right. If you occupy a position with any visibility, you're always giving a "performance" where others are concerned. And most of the time, they're a rapt audience!

Exercise 17: Grounding

Ancient actors knew that part of their power in performance came from the earth itself (for today's actors, it's the stage floor). That's because in the earliest forms of Western theater in ancient Greece, actors performed outside, as the Greek amphitheaters were built into a hillside. Visualize a ballet dancer's leap upward and you'll understand that the same need for the earth's power then applies to today's performers: the energy for all forms of theatrical action originates from the earth under our feet.

When you *ground yourself* in meetings, conversations while standing at trade shows, meeting someone for the first time, or delivering a pitch or presentation, you acquire the same power and connection to the earth as those ancient tragedians and comedians. The steadfastness and sense of purpose you then display is instantly noticeable to anyone and everyone. Consequently, you'll be showing the exact opposite of nerves, self-consciousness, and self-doubt.

Sound mysterious? Actually, it couldn't be simpler.

You ground yourself by standing firmly on the earth (or in your case, the floor) in a strong rather than a weak position.

Practice it now:

- Stand straight with your feet firmly planted on the floor at armpit or shoulder width. And "plant" is the perfect word! Imagine that you're a 300-year-old oak tree with roots that go deep and wide into the earth. Like that tree, you are firm, secure, and unshakeable.

- For one moment, intentionally *weaken* your strong stance by standing with your legs crossed, then leaning on one hip, then standing with your feet touching (like a toy tin soldier), or any other habit you may have that puts you off-balance. You can easily see how these common stances can weaken anyone's impression of you, since in visual terms, it seems like any challenge or resistance will blow you over!

- Now ground yourself again, with both feet flat and at a stable width. Actually feel your feet gripping the floor through your shoes. Did something just happen to your self-image? I bet it did! If you were someone else looking at this person (you), does it almost seem like he or she is holding their ground?

Develop a habit of standing this way. (Do it when you're sitting as well, with the same sense of a strong yet comfortable stance with your feet planted on the floor.) An interesting thing can happen when you ground yourself: *other physical expressions of confidence* may begin to emerge. Allow this self-regulating cycle of physical strength and confidence to become part of your persona.

Here's a true story of how just a few minutes of grounding helped someone cope with a stressful situation:

Some years ago, I conducted a lunch-and-learn workshop for the women's networking group of a Boston-area Chamber of Commerce. As part of my workshop, I took a volunteer from the audience to demonstrate the importance of breathing, body language, and other aspects of nonverbal communication for speakers. The young woman who volunteered was obviously nervous, but good for her...she gave it a go!

She spoke for around five minutes on the topic I suggested: her nonprofit organization's mission in the community. I then coached her for no more than a few minutes on how to overcome her nervousness. I showed her how to slow down and deepen her breathing, and then to ground herself, as in the exercise you just completed. She improved at once. Her level of confidence and competence seemed to grow right in front of everyone, as the other women in the group all testified.

A few weeks later, I received a lovely email from the young woman telling me about how helpful she found that exercise. She was the maid of honor at her cousin's wedding, and had to speak at the reception. She was very nervous, and had been worrying that she wouldn't do a good job and would somehow spoil her cousin's special day. Then, she said, she remembered to ground herself so she was standing strongly, and to breathe diaphragmatically to take control of the moment. "Immediately," she wrote, "I calmed down and felt like I was completely present for my toast. It went wonderfully. Thank you for helping me that day at the workshop!"

You can experience exactly the same benefit by combining the deep-rooted sense of presence you just practiced in "grounding" with the diaphragmatic breathing discussed earlier in this book. These techniques don't have anything in particular to do with public speaking, though as we have just seen, they can be transformative for a speaker who is nervous or anxious. They will *always* work for you, whatever the situation. They are essential tools in getting to know your own body, and they can help you tap into your physical presence to project control, confidence, and competence.

Exercise 18: The Body Language Checklists

Your body is not only an extremely important tool in terms of interacting with others; it's also a vital part of your sense of self-confidence. When you "broadcast" confidence physically, those you deal with will react to you positively. That, in turn, gives you confidence that the situation is under control and, in fact, you are doing well. Thus, confidence leads directly to more confidence!

Below are two checklists you can use to make sure you're displaying confidence while adding appropriate physical expressiveness to what you say. They are equally applicable to both personal and professional settings and situations.

WAS MY BODY LANGUAGE EFFECTIVE AS A COMMUNICATION TOOL?

- ☑ Did I appear confident yet relaxed?
- ☑ Did I use natural movements while avoiding repetitive gestures?
- ☑ Did my gestures amplify the points I was making?

☑ Was my face expressive of my ideas and emotions?

☑ Did I make direct and ongoing eye contact?

USE OF SPACE: DID I COMMAND THE SPACE IN WHICH I MOVED?

☑ Did I "own" my space, using the area for physical movement?

☑ Were my movement and gestures fluid rather than abrupt or jerky?

☑ Did I sit or stand poised without slouching?

☑ Was I open physically and not closed off in any way?

☑ Was I animated instead of appearing stiff and wooden?

NOTES

1 Brian Stelter, "8 Hours a Day Spent on Screens, Study Finds," New York Times, March 27, 2009.

CHAPTER 5

Mindfulness and Living Fully In the Moment

The exercises in this chapter teach you an approach to mindfulness through meditation *that will help you be fully present in the moment*. In a very real way, these exercises reintroduce you to the world around you and how you are responding to it.

It may seem odd, but the truth is that most of us almost never practice that kind of presence. Obviously, if you're a person who is good at always being present and whose energy seems plugged into the moment as it unfolds, you'll impress people and connect with them easily. Also, of course, being in that state means you *won't* be focused on your fears and anxieties and worrying about how you're doing.

There's also the fact that as you go about your day, you're partly in the past in your thoughts and partly in the future (both of which you can't do anything about at the moment). Behaving like this is just part of being human. On the other hand, the more you can participate fully in the present moment and process it in real time, the more empowered you'll be. And those you're interacting with will benefit from being with someone (you!) who zeros in on what needs to be said or done *at the moment.*

This chapter is all about showing you how to stay calm, centered, and focused so you can take a giant step toward that kind of presence. The first exercise, "Focused Relaxation," is about remaining relaxed and focused at the same time while minimizing intrusive thoughts. The six other exercises in the chapter all have you *doing* something as the mechanism for reaching a meditative state.

These exercises also open up your mind to new sensory experiences, as you become much more aware of the essence of an activity—what it involves and your part in it. Sensory exercises like these can be real eye-openers (literally and otherwise). I'll tell you what I mean.

I trained as an actor at the Webber Douglas Academy of Dramatic Art in London. A class exercise there in the type of sensory perception I'm talking about above really allowed me to understand the value of "opening up one's senses." In class one day, the Acting Studies instructor gave each of us a small object. We were told to examine the object we'd just been given without any preconceptions whatsoever of what it was or how it worked. In other words, we were to wipe out from our memory what this thing was and what it did, and examine it as if we had never seen such a thing before.

I was given a pencil. So, for me, the exercise involved examining a thin wooden, painted and glazed object that was smooth but hexagonal, that is, it had six sides. One end of it came to a sharp point where something that looked like a soft mineral emerged from the wood. The other end had a rubbery substance attached. This was puzzling, because whatever the rubbery substance was for seemed pretty much the opposite of what the sharp end's job was. And so on.

When you go through an exercise like this, you become acutely aware of what your senses are revealing to you. Your *imagination* leaps into life, going from 0 to 60 faster than any race car. Waking up your imagination like this is part of the exercises that follow here as well.

Think of it this way: when you *invest* yourself fully in something while letting other considerations and thoughts slip away, that activity begins to pay rapid dividends. For instance, the following exercise, "Focused Relaxation" pays off in three distinct and valuable ways. I'll discuss each of them after you've finished the exercise.

So, here you go:

Exercise 19: Focused Relaxation

1. This is a 5-minute exercise. I suggest that you set a timer that will let you know when that amount of time is up.

2. Find a quiet solitary place. Sit comfortably in a well-supported position, feet flat on the floor.

3. Close your eyes.

4. "Listen" to your breath for the first minute. Pay attention to what happens when you breathe in slowly and calmly. Understand *with your body* rather than your mind how breathing nourishes and sustains you. Feel the breath flow down your throat, filling your

lungs then bringing life-giving oxygen to every cell of your body.

5. Now, focus your awareness on a visual image you "see" in your mind. Make it a simple shape in a neutral color without any emotional overtones: a green circle, a yellow square, a blue triangle, etc. Avoid the color red with its associations of passion and blood; and likewise, stay away from any shape that is a symbol or has meaning apart from the shape itself.

6. *See* that object in your mind's eye: color and shape—a yellow circle, say. Bring it to the best level of clarity that you can. Don't worry if you find this difficult. It takes considerable concentration and focus to see both a shape and its color. For instance, you might succeed in visualizing one but not the other. But keep at it. If you don't succeed on your first try, you might see your object more clearly the second time you try it. Remember, like any other activity, you'll eventually get good at it if you give it your best shot every time.

7. As you work at making your colored shape appear in your mind's eye, images, thoughts, and feelings may rise in your consciousness, or you may become aware of sounds around you. Notice them but don't latch onto them; simply let them these thoughts continue on their way, or accept the presence of the sound. Bring your focus back to your image. *Do* nothing; just let your awareness *be*.

8. Your breathing will become slower and deeper. It's okay to notice that; but keep trying to bring your colored shape into view. If you've succeeded in doing so by this time, *keep* the shape there in front of you. At this point, you should be in a calmer and more concentrated frame of mind: a state of "focused relaxation," whether or not you've succeeded in seeing the yellow circle you were aiming for.

9. *Feel* this state of focused relaxation. Do you see how both words apply? To be fully relaxed yet focused feels pretty good, doesn't it? When the five minutes is up, open your eyes and slowly stand. Notice with your mind *and* your body what this new state feels like. Maintain this level of calm focus and healthy, deeper breathing as you go about your daily tasks.

How did that feel for you? Take a moment now and debrief your own experience: Did you achieve the combination of calmness and convergence the exercise aims for? Were you able to "see" a well-defined colored shape? Was it difficult to maintain your focus because of intrusive thoughts? Whatever areas you found challenging in this exercise are the very ones you should practice to get better at.

Now let's analyze why "Focused Relaxation" is a valuable exercise for overcoming fear and anxiety while countering negative or intrusive thoughts. I mentioned that there were three benefits to the exercise. Here they are:

Benefit #1: It teaches you that you can control your breathing.
As you just experienced, this exercise slows your breathing down

as you enter a semi-meditative state. You learned in Chapter 3 that the vagus nerve is responsible for slowing down your heart rate each time you exhale. "Focused Relaxation" does this for you *automatically* as soon as you allow yourself to enter the focused meditation called for in the exercise. It's really sleight-of-hand: Concentrating on a shape you want to see in your mind's eye, (rather than on your breathing), allows you to experience a slower respiration cycle without even trying to do so! You already know that your breathing quickly becomes rapid and shallow when you're fearful or you feel anxious (the link with PTSD). The exercise shows you how to get into a groove of slower and more relaxed respiration. When (not *if*) you get good at it, you'll have a handy exercise right in your back pocket to get you into a calmer state in just 5 minutes!

Benefit #2: It builds up your "focus muscle" (as I call this imaginary structure in the brain). A more confident you is the one who attends to the task at hand, instead of being distressed or perhaps even avoiding the task. So, anything that helps improve your mental focus is good. As you now know, this exercise challenges you quite a bit in demanding that you see both the color *and* shape of your imaginary object. By accepting the challenge, you're getting valuable practice in learning how to achieve stronger focus. And anyway, the fact that you did take up the challenge should give you confidence!

Benefit #3: It teaches you not to listen to harmful self-talk. This is a big one, and it may be the most beneficial aspect of the exercise. We all experience random thoughts when we're trying to concentrate on something. It's part of our nature. As I said above: *notice these thoughts but don't latch onto them; simply* *let them continue on their way as they float through your mind.*

Yes, they may be harmless thoughts. But they may instead be part of the self-criticism you routinely inflict upon yourself. Many people do so. In either case, you mustn't stop what you're trying to do—in this case, seeing your colored shape—to follow that butterfly (or anvil) of a thought. And you can't say, "I WON'T PAY ANY ATTENTION TO YOU, THOUGHT!" because you surely will. The trick is simply to notice that you are having this thought…before you let it slide quietly on its way. Back to focus. Back to the task at hand.

THE MINDFULNESS EXERCISES

In the Acknowledgment at the beginning of this book, you may have noticed the term "mindfulness." It's a word you've probably heard or read about before. You should be clear on what is meant by the term, however, as six exercises for mindfulness follow, below, for you to try.

Although the term is generally associated with modern Buddhist philosophy, according to the *Oxford English Dictionary* the word has been around since 1561 (as "mindfulnesse"), and in its present form since 1817.[1] The concept is simple yet profound: mindfulness means being fully attentive to the here-and-now, i.e., completely in the present moment and attuned to your surroundings.

Consider how far this state is from being consumed with anxiety, fear, or lack of confidence in a difficult situation! When you are in such a state, you run the risk of being disconnected from everything except what you're thinking and feeling about yourself. When that happens, you aren't living in the present moment at all but in the *future*, when this painful experience (whatever it is) will be over.

How to Achieve Mindfulness. The key to achieving mindfulness is to make it a daily habit. If you can become more mindful in *everything* you do, you'll make things much easier for yourself in situations where your concentration is most at risk.

Below are six exercises to help you attain mindfulness on a daily basis. All except the last one (which is my own) are from Thich Nhat Hanh's book, *The Miracle of Mindfulness.* Try one or two of these exercises today; and perhaps two others tomorrow. Remember that like all habits, mindfulness takes time to attain. Yet the benefits for both your public and private life are undeniable.

Exercise 20: The Half-Smile

Just as moods and feelings are reflected in your body language and facial expressions, by assuming a physical pose or look on your face, you can *call up* a particular feeling. That's because your mind and body have a lifetime's worth of experience in connecting thoughts and emotions to what you're showing the world. "Wearing a smile" is one way you can accomplish this goal.

Smile and the World Smiles With You: Take hold of your breath. Inhale and exhale three breaths gently while maintaining a half-smile. Now "follow your breath" as it makes its way down your throat or nasal passage and out to all the parts of your body.

You can do this literally anywhere you find yourself, at any time. Put on a half-smile. Inhale and exhale quietly three times. Maintain the half-smile as you go about your day.

Exercise 21: Making Tea

Mindfulness While Making Tea: Prepare a pot of tea to serve to guests or to yourself. Do each movement slowly and purpose-fully—be *mindful* of it. Do not let one detail of your movements go by that you are not mindful of. Know that your hand lifts the pot by its handle. Know that you are pouring the fragrant warm tea into the cup. Take each step in mindfulness. Breathe gently and a bit more deeply than usual. If your mind strays, take hold of your breath again; your mind will follow.

[Note: In Japan, the tea ceremony—known as *sadō* or *chadō* or "the way of the tea"—is a tradition that has been celebrated for five hundred years. You might get an idea of why it is helpful for our purpose of using meditation to calm and center yourself by reading this sentence: "Beyond just serving and receiving tea, one of the main purposes of the tea ceremony is for the guests to enjoy the hospitality of the host in an atmosphere distinct from the fast pace of everyday life."[2]]

Exercise 22: Washing the Dishes

The Importance of Washing the Dishes: Wash the dishes in a state of composure and relaxation. Treat each plate or dish as an object of contemplation. Consider each bowl as sacred. Follow your breath to prevent your mind from straying. Do not try to hurry to get the job over with. Consider washing the dishes the most important thing in life. Washing the dishes is meditation. If you cannot wash the dishes in mindfulness, neither can you meditate while sitting in silence.

Exercise 23: A Slow-Motion Bath

Enjoy a Long, Slow Bath: Allow yourself 30 to 45 minutes to take a bath. Don't hurry for even one second. From the moment you prepare the bathwater to the moment you put on clean clothes, let every motion be light and slow. Be attentive of every movement. Place your attention on every part of your body, without discrimination or fear. Be mindful of each stream of water on your body. By the time you've finished, your mind should feel as peaceful and light as your body. Follow your breath. Think of yourself as being in a clean and fragrant lotus pond in the summer (or perhaps for those of us in the West, a forest pond or the old watering hole!).

Exercise 24: Yourself

Understand How You Are Connected to Everything: Sit in a dark room by yourself, or alone by a river at night, or anywhere else where there is solitude. Begin to take hold of your breath. Give rise to the thought, "I will use my finger to point at myself," and then instead of pointing at your body, point away in the opposite direction. Contemplate seeing yourself outside of your bodily form. There it is: in the trees, the grass and leaves, the river. Be mindful that you are in the universe and the universe is in you: if the universe is, you are; if you are, the universe is. There is no birth. There is no death. There is no coming. There is no going. Maintain the half-smile. Take hold of your breath. Contemplate for 10 to 20 minutes.

Exercise 25: Taking a Walk

Notice the World Around You: Take a few moments now to *reintroduce yourself to the world.* Go for a walk in the early morning or evening. Whatever you do, don't think about business or social issues that you know have a tendency to tie you in a knot. This is your personal time. If you can imagine a time clock, you've just heard the sound of your card "clocking" you out.

What you *do* want to focus on is being outside in the fresh air, and breathing it all in. An entire world is passing slowly by as you walk. Notice it. Calmly contemplate the things around you of the earth and the air. If there is water nearby, watch and listen to it. Try to do this every day for at least a half-hour.

Perhaps you noticed the slowness and deliberateness present in all of these exercises. This in itself is a reminder that when you hurry through tasks, you can't fully appreciate what you're doing, i.e., you are not living fully in the moment. In a way, you lose yourself in this process as well!

NOTES

1   Oxford English Dictionary, 2nd ed., 2002, as reported at http:// en.wikipedia.org/wiki/Mindfulness_%28 Buddhism%29.

2   https://wisdomanswer.com/what-is-the-purpose-of-a-tea-ceremony/

CHAPTER 6

Changing Your Negative Thinking

In Shakespeare's most famous play, Hamlet tells the character Rosencrantz: "There is nothing either good or bad, but thinking makes it so." It's a statement that has some truth in it concerning your own thoughts about your fears, anxieties, and lack of confidence.

In one sense, you create your own fearful responses to the situations that are difficult for you. That is because, almost universally, there is never as much danger or risk as you think there is concerning an encounter. But your anxiety leads you down a path with no exit, since you're substituting your fears for more accurate measures to judge both the difficulties and the possibilities of your success or failure. And so you create a false reality that's really much harsher than the actual situation.

In this chapter, you'll work on changing such unprofitable thinking. You'll learn how to change unhealthy thoughts into healthy and constructive ones. You'll banish the negative self-talk that's been undermining your achievements by building a repertoire of positive coping statements instead. And you'll discover how to evaluate what you say and do (especially to yourself) more realistically, using more realistic measures of your progress.

Is that a lot to accomplish in one chapter? Maybe. But you'll be able to do it. That's because restructuring negative thinking is a key activity in overcoming anxiety—and no one knows as much about your own negative thoughts as you do.

This process, of re-routing negative thinking into productive channels is called COGNITIVE RESTRUCTURING. It simply means what it sounds like: re-configuring or restructuring your thoughts and self-talk. It involves taking them from negative territory to positive ground where you can more accurately judge the difficulties you face and how you can overcome them. Another way to say this is: *you'll be changing your role from being your own worst enemy to becoming your own best friend.*

ARE YOU BIASED AGAINST YOURSELF?
Karen: A Case Study

Karen is a 36-year-old Senior Learning Manager for a leading computer manufacturer. She conducts in-house workshops worldwide for IT managers on the software that her company sells. She came to me a little less than a year ago because, she said, "I'm a horrible presenter!" Not only did she believe that she had no talent for speaking in public. She was also sure that she was broadcasting that fact to her trainees.

In Karen's mind, it was only a matter of time before her firm's management discovered the awful truth about her lack of skills and let her go. So she was a bundle of nerves: terrified of conducting the training workshops that were the core of her job, while to her own thinking she was "living a lie" and was constantly on the verge of being found out.

Note Karen's response to her public speaking assignments: She *believed* that she had no talent for the task. She was *certain* everyone else realized it too. And she *knew* therefore that she was living a lie as a supposedly competent training professional. Clearly, Karen's own cognitive process was a major stumbling block to her job satisfaction and feelings of self-worth! It was time to restructure her cognition (via cognitive restructuring).

Naturally, Karen desperately wanted to improve what she considered inferior abilities as a trainer and presenter. But as I pointed out to her, before she could get to that point, she had to change her thinking. As I told her, starting out with feelings of negative self-worth is the weakest possible position from which to build dynamic communication skills.

* * *

Let's take Karen's situation and apply it to the general population of people who are anxious about their abilities. After all, feelings like hers are common among people who believe they're simply average or worse as social communicators or practitioners of their profession.

One of the biggest challenges anxious people like Karen face is that they overestimate how negatively others will judge them. The truth, of course, is that most people we talk to and interact with aren't picking apart our abilities or personalities. Instead, they're looking for something positive from the experience—they're actually focused on the message or the information being conveyed.

But if you're thinking about how poorly you're doing in the encounter, you're too busy monitoring what you consider to be your own poor performance to understand that.

You're biased against yourself! You may, in fact, be doing quite well. But you spoil your success by creating "a negative reality." Then you reinforce your belief that you're doing badly through self-criticism…even if you've actually succeeded at your goal! You might even say that you're determined to be miserable despite your success.

Does any of this sound familiar to you? If it does, you need to make the commitment *not* to indulge in self-talk like this that's clearly counter-productive to your success and feelings of well-being.

Exercise 26: Overcoming Worst-Case Thinking

Clearly, if, like Karen, you indulge in a belief that you're worthless or at least lacking in key skills, you need to align yourself more closely with reality. After all, people most likely do enjoy interacting with you, and you're probably gainfully employed. One way to be more realistic about what might happen in an anxiety-provoking situation is by *overcoming worst-case thinking.*

Worst-case thinking means imagining that a truly awful outcome is going to occur despite little or no evidence that that's the case. For instance, if the plane you're on tips to one side because of strong winds, worst-case thinking makes you wonder if one of the engines just quit. If you have a headache, worst-case thinking tells you it might be the first symptom of a brain tumor. You may be delighted to have been selected to deliver a keynote speech, but you're also sure *something* bad is going to happen when the whole company or all of the conference attendees are looking at you.

Ridiculous, isn't it? Yet egged on by performance anxiety,

you may happily buy into such fantasies. And even if you don't really think, say, the stage is going to collapse as you approach the podium, your brain is whispering, "Well it *could!*" The truth is, you're "awfulizing" in the most unproductive way imaginable.

Worst-case thinking saps your mental energy as it keeps you focused in the wrong direction, i.e., on bad things that aren't going to happen. You can't think about the good things (or even the normal things) that are more likely to occur!

The exercise on the next page, "Overcoming Worst-Case Thinking," is designed to point your thoughts in the right direction rather than down those dead-end alleyways.

Here's how to do the exercise:

Jot down in the first column ("Event or situation") some situations that are typical for you. These can be events coming up or ones you participated in in the past, especially if you experienced some worst-case thinking regarding them. In the second column ("Worst-case scenario"), go ahead and write down the type of awful outcomes you're prone to imagine. Don't worry about being realistic—that's not the object of this exercise. Just let those wild imaginings about possible disasters come out!

The next two columns are for you to come back down to earth. The third column ("Evidence that the worst-case scenario will or did take place") asks for any actual *evidence* that such catastrophes will occur or did occur. And the last column ("More likely outcome") prompts you to record the more probable outcome in terms of what usually happens or would be *most likely* to happen in each situation.

Okay…blast away!

OVERCOMING WORST-CASE THINKING

Event or situation	Worst-case scenario	Evidence that the worst-case scenario will or did take place	More likely outcome

Now look over what you've got.

Is your evidence for an awful outcome on each occasion (column three) looking a bit sparse?

Isn't it true that the last column—the "more likely outcome"—is closer to reality by a country mile? So aren't *those* the situations you should be preparing for, bringing to them a more realistic attitude and higher level of confidence?

Exercise 27: Developing Positive Coping Statements

As the previous exercise demonstrates, *it's as easy to deal with reality as it is to dwell on situations that aren't likely to occur.* The next step in cognitive restructuring is equally important. It involves changing your negative self-talk into positive coping statements.

Have you heard the term "self-fulfilling prophecy"? It means to dwell on something (like an unpleasant or unwanted outcome) so much, or so frequently, that the event comes to pass as you imagined it. The German philosopher Friedrich Nietzsche, for instance, famously said that if you stare into the abyss long enough the abyss stares back at you. It's no different with the things you do and dwell on: if you think negative thoughts consistently enough, they become your mantra. And if you regularly direct your energies toward those negative outcomes, isn't there a good chance that at least some of them will occur?

Creating NEGATIVE SELF-FULFILLING PROPHECIES like this is a popular activity among people who suffer from anxiety. Here's what I tell clients who exhibit this behavior: If you're going to spend time and energy dwelling on a situation or event, why not think *positively* about it rather than negatively? You'll expend the same amount of time and mental energy, so it doesn't take any more effort. And which prophecy do you want to come true, after all: a successful outcome or a failure?

The exercise that follows, "Developing Positive Coping Statements," will help get you into the right mindset about all of this. In this exercise, you'll be pairing examples of some of your negative self-talk with more positive statements you come up with on the same issue. Some of the negative self-talk given in the first column may be actual statements you already make to yourself. If that's true, you can immediately start using the Positive Coping Statements in the opposite column (the two contrasting statements are linked in every case). Below the examples I've provided is space for you to write *your* favorite self-undermining statements!

By accepting and repeating your new positive coping statements instead (out loud), you'll be creating a *new mantra* which will point you not toward failure but success. It's a simple yet powerful way to change your habitual negative thinking process and to build confidence!

Developing Positive Coping Statements

Negative Self-Talk	Positive Coping Statement
I'm just not good at my job (or this task).	I can learn the skills of being effective at this.
People can see I'm not confident.	It's okay to be nervous. And most of it doesn't show, anyway.
I'm going to look like a fool.	My goal is all about getting my message across well.
It's going to be a disaster.	This is a great opportunity for a productive encounter!
Lots of things could go wrong.	I'm prepared and ready. This should go well.
This is a make-or-break situation.	Even if it doesn't go great, it's not the end of the world.
These people will judge me.	I know what I'm talking about, and they will see that.
What have I gotten myself into?	What do I have to lose?

Everyone's going to be looking at me!	It's great to have this level of visibility!
I'm going to go blank—I know it.	I can speak knowledgeably on this topic whatever occurs.
They'll ask me something I don't know.	Of course. Someone always does. I'll admit it. Then find out.
I have to be perfect.	I need to be good, not perfect. Nobody is. Here goes.

ASSESSING YOUR PROGRESS IN THIS CHAPTER SO FAR

You should feel good about the pair of exercises you just completed. You're already building a toolbox of helpful strategies to replace negative thinking that may be undermining your confidence. For instance:

- You now know how to restructure your negative thinking, with the help of two tried-and-true techniques: "Overcoming Worst-Case Thinking," and "Developing Positive Coping Statements."

- Through these exercises, you've begun getting in touch with the reality of the situations you find yourself in, rather than focusing on unlikely events that have little chance of occurring.

- You're turning negative self-talk into statements that reinforce a healthy and positive attitude toward yourself.

With the next exercise, you're going to go one step further. And it's an important step. You're going to transform yourself from someone trying to *survive* difficult situations, into someone who uses self-expression as a tool for dynamic communication.
Ready?
Away you go…

Exercise 28: Channeling Your Thinking — 10 Statements

This exercise features two techniques for *channeling your thinking* in the right direction. You'll do so by (1) taking a constructive rather than a destructive approach to the situations you face; and (2) using spoken repetition.

In "Channeling Your Thinking," you'll create verbal patterns that you repeat to yourself. The patterns will be simple ones. Yet they'll take you all the way from vocalized self-doubt to preparing yourself to succeed every time you speak.

To begin, select a negative statement you typically use concerning your own ability. You'll see some examples in the exercise. (Note that these statements aren't as concerned with specific outcomes as was the negative self-talk featured in the previous exercise. These statements are more concerned with your idea of your overall abilities as a professional.) Be honest with yourself regarding the things you actually say to yourself that undermine your confidence.

Next, you'll make that same statement *less negative* by softening it a bit. Finally, you'll turn it around completely into a *positive and affirming statement* about your ability.

Once you've created this sequence of three statements—negative, less negative, and positive—*say the statements aloud* 10 times, reading across the page from left to right. Then go down to the second series of three statements and say those aloud 10 times, and so on down the page.

What's the idea behind this exercise? Well, if you *think* something, that's nice—you may remember it or not. If you *think it and then write it down*, it's more likely to stick. And if you *think it, write it down, then say it out loud (repeatedly)*, you'll really be helping to cement that positive statement in your consciousness. This exercise has you do all three.

The first three examples are already given to you. Below that, write seven of your own examples of negative statements. These should be ones you're in the habit of making that need to be changed into positive statements. (You know what they are!)

The 10-10-10 Pattern

Negative statement	Less negative statement	Positive statement
1. I'm a loser.	I'm not a loser.	I'm a winner.
2. I'm a poor communicator.	I'm okay at communicating.	I'm a good communicator.
3. It's clear I lack confidence.	I shouldn't display self-doubt.	People will see I'm confident.
4.		
5.		
6.		
7.		
8.		
9.		
10.		

Did you remember to say all of your sequences of statements aloud, ten times each?

Good—now you're ready to move on to the "10-10" Pattern. In this version, using the same statements you've already written, you'll go directly from your negative statement into positive territory by eliminating the middleman. Again, repeat each two-statement sequence aloud 10 times across the page, then move down to the next statement. Use the same statements you wrote above for numbers 4 through 10.

The 10-10-10 Pattern

Negative statement	Positive statement
I'm a loser.	I'm a winner.
I'm a poor communicator.	I'm a good communicator.
It's clear I lack confidence.	People will see I'm confident.

Exercise 29: Know Where You're Going!

Congratulations! By taking part in the previous two exercises, you've not only practiced going from self-doubt about your abilities to positive affirmations. You've also given yourself a tool that has these further benefits:

1. You've created positive statements (the right-hand column) that you can use as a mantra before you speak.

2. *Hearing* yourself say productive things out loud is reinforcement of a favorable mindset.

DEFINING YOUR GOALS APART FROM YOUR ANXIETY AND FEARS

It's well worth keeping in mind the following: just as you shouldn't measure your success in any professional encounter by whether you were anxious or not,* you shouldn't set your goals along the same lines.

> * *What matters, of course, is how much the* stakeholders *benefitted from what you said.*

You should always aim toward giving the people you're dealing with the clearest version of the important message you're there to deliver. Your goal is *always* to give them the thing of value that they need—whether they themselves realize they need it or not. It's entirely possible, for instance, for you to be filled with self-doubt yet conclude a transaction successfully. A real-life example: one of my clients is a commercial real estate salesman of office space in downtown Boston. He shared with me the time that he considered his pitch to an important corporate team to be rocky and not at all up to his standards. That day, however, he'd ended up leasing *three floors* in an office high-rise to that firm!

Similarly, your long-term objectives can't be defined by whether you've overcome your lack of self-confidence, or even your nervousness in certain situations. Striving to make the statement true that "My aim is to be a much more confident individual" is too self-limiting in terms of your overall professional goals. While it's important—even vital—to be able to control your anxiety and fears, your ultimate goals should still be concerned with what you want to achieve in your position, for your organization, or whatever other metrics are important to you. (The same is true of your personal and social goals.)

It's just something to bear in mind so that you don't place all of your focus on overcoming your deficits, instead of *making that simply a part of pursuing your greater goals.*

Know where you're going!

* * *

One more thing: always be aware of the need to define your objectives clearly. *That's* the basis of knowing whether you've succeeded or not.

Here are some examples of ineffective versus effective objectives. The latter *must* be measurable in some way from your performance:

INEFFECTIVE OBJECTIVE:

To inform the sales force about the new software that they will be selling to our customers.

EFFECTIVE OBJECTIVE:

To train each participant on the new software, and make sure everyone gets the right answers on the test questions.

INEFFECTIVE OBJECTIVE:

To bring the lab team up to speed on how our new seed line will result in much greater crop yields.

EFFECTIVE OBJECTIVE:

To demonstrate through the data from our recent field tests showing that the new seed line results in a 50% increase in crop yields.

INEFFECTIVE OBJECTIVE:

To convince potential investors that this fund is rock-solid and should allow them to recoup their initial investment in a favorable timeframe.

EFFECTIVE OBJECTIVE:

To show how if the projected sales figures are met investors should recoup their initial investment in this fund in 3 years.

Notice how each of the effective objectives uses the infinitive form of a verb: *to train*; *to demonstrate*; *to show*. These are action-based words that will help define your success in the endeavor in your own mind. And if you do that, of course, you'll have a much greater chance of defining that same success in the stakeholders' minds.

You can also easily see how these objectives exist entirely outside of your personal concerns and anxieties. By using such empirical tools, you can link your actions with an objective evaluation of whether those actions would be successful (and afterwards, if they *were* successful).

By defining your objectives clearly, that is, you'll more easily know when you accomplish them. Adding this approach to the other exercises in this chapter, you'll go a long way toward changing your destructive thinking about your abilities—in particular, going from "negative self-talk" to confidence-building positive coping statements.

CHAPTER 7

Using Positive Visualization

Do you golf? Ski? Enjoy chess? When you're about to have a serious discussion with your spouse or your boss, do you imagine how the conversation will go? Or when you're driving home at night, do you anticipate in your mind's eye that curve in the road you know is ahead so you can slow down in time?

In these situations and others, chances are you *visualize* the best way to proceed to give yourself an edge.

To be successful in your personal and professional endeavors, you can benefit from using the exact same technique. Visualizing giving an effective presentation, say, makes it much easier to achieve that result. As I often say to clients: If you're going to spend the time and energy to think ahead about an upcoming event, why not make your effort productive instead of destructive? That is, why worry and imagine negative outcomes that may not occur unless you *help* them happen! (See the previous chapter on changing your negative thinking.)

One of the best ways to do so is through a technique called POSITIVE VISUALIZATION. This chapter explains the technique and gives you some opportunities to practice.

Let's look at how positive visualization works:

THE POWER OF A SELF-FULFILLING PROPHECY

Do you know about the white lines on the highway? — When you're driving, one of the worst things you can do is to focus on the painted lines in the center of the road. If you stare at those lines long enough, you'll begin drifting *toward* them, i.e., close to or into the path of oncoming traffic. By directing your energy and attention toward the lines, you'll have created an *attraction* between you and them. After that, it's just a case of you following your attraction.

Another way to say this is, *when you create the right conditions for something to occur, it's much more likely for that outcome to take place.* In effect, you're preparing for the event subconsciously and getting yourself ready to respond to it.

Now consider all of this in terms of your work and personal relationships. When you have something important coming up, naturally you think about it a lot. Even if you're not particularly anxious concerning the outcome, you'll still give it plenty of "mind time." And if you're prone to anxiety or lack of confidence, chances are you'll create negative scenarios about what's going to take place.

In other words, you're in danger of creating a self-fulfilling prophecy, in this case on the negative side. By establishing the right conditions, you're heading toward—and in a sense, inviting—the very outcome you don't want to occur!

You should also know that this is not a passive process. It takes a lot of work to undermine yourself! But if you recognize the nature of self-fulfilling prophecies and accept your own power to head them off, you can put yourself back on the path to success.

The following pages offer seven exercises to help you do so. These scenarios—all of which use positive visualization—are specifically designed to "lighten your load" in terms of anxiety and to place you in a more positive frame of mind.

From there, it's just a case of allowing the beneficial outcomes to take place!

Exercise 30: The Mini-Vacation

This activity is an excellent continuation of the benefits you gained in the "Progressive Relaxation" exercise from Chapter 1. It can also be done on its own.

Its value is twofold: First, it associates your experience of past pleasure with a state of relaxation in the present. And second, it awakens your sensory apparatus to the world around you. It's therefore a very enjoyable and valuable activity!

- Lie on your back, with your eyes closed and arms and feet uncrossed at your sides.

- Follow your breath, as previously. Allow your body to relish each life-giving, delicious breath. Give yourself over to your breathing. Let it fill your consciousness.

- Focus your awareness on the present time and place: the here-and-now: your office, the den or living room at home, the hotel room you're staying in, wherever you happen to be trying this exercise. Think about where you are. Listen to the sounds around you. Smell the air in this space. Become aware of the floor underneath you and the sensation of the air on your skin. Does this place have any taste associated with it? See in your mind's eye what this room looks like. (You're using all five of your senses as you experience this time and setting.) For a few minutes, fill yourself completely with this sensory input. Now, imagine that the reality of this place and time is slowly dissolving, melting away into nothingness.

- In its place, you find yourself traveling to a favorite location—someplace where you love to go. This place is now becoming clear in your consciousness. It might be a beach on a warm summer day; a field in springtime; a hammock outdoors in the early autumn; a cozy fire in a ski lodge at the end of a day on the slopes. Perhaps you're lying in the bottom of a rowboat that's bobbing gently at the dock. Wherever you are, this is now your new reality, and you're relaxing here.

- Open yourself up completely to this special place. Experience it *sensually*, as you did a moment ago in the present time and location. What sounds are you hearing now on your mini-vacation? Seagulls? Waves slapping at the bottom of the boat? Bees buzzing? A crackling fire? Imagine (visualize) the heat from the sun plus the breeze on your face as you lie in the field, or the warmth of the fire at the ski lodge. Are there any smells noticeable in this place? If you were to open your eyes, what would you see? Do you taste anything—the salty air at the beach or the smoky air in front of the fire? Allow your senses to feed you the entirety of this world that you've recreated.

- Spend the next five or ten minutes enjoying this place. Take it all in deeply. Then slowly let it too begin to dissolve in your consciousness. In its place, bring back the present time and location where you're doing this exercise. *But keep the level of deep relaxation and sensory awareness you experienced on your "vacation."* The present time and place is the same as it was before, except now you're experiencing it much more fully. Let it flood into you and throughout you.

- When you're ready, open your eyes. While staying completely relaxed, sit up slowly (no need to rush). Relish the sensations of the renewed here-and-now you're bathing in.

- Now take this feeling with you as you go about your tasks for the rest of the day. Keep the relaxation of your mini-vacation not only in your mind, but also in all of your senses and in your body—i.e., your physical response to the world around you.

FOLLOW-UP: Did you notice how important your *sensory experience* was in this exercise? Whether you were in your present location or in your vacation spot, your world should have been filled with sensory input: sound, smell, touch, taste, and (even with your eyes closed) the sights of the place you were actually in or imagined you were visiting.

By the end of the exercise, you may even have achieved a new level of awareness concerning the input of your physical senses. Good! In a way, you're more alive to the world now. This is a very valuable skill to have if you're feeling isolated and removed from the present moment because of anxiety! People who can immerse themselves in the present and experience it fully have a great advantage when it comes to achieving calmness and a feeling of being centered and tuned-in to *this* moment. If you can do that, you can bet that you will increase your sense of self-confidence, as well as your listeners' confidence in you.

Exercise 31: The Balloon Man/Lady

In this exercise, you'll start by filling yourself up with…

Nothing.

That's right: imagine a feeling of complete emptiness, with not even air inside you! Notice how utterly light this makes you feel. You're no longer burdened down by weighty matters of *any* kind. You're now light enough, in fact, to float away….

What you're experiencing is not just playfulness but a serious concept from Zen Buddhism, which aims to "liberate us from all the yokes under which we finite beings are usually suffering in this world."[1]

The particular burden you're attempting to get out from under, of course, is your anxiety. Weighty thoughts, heavy breathing, a sense of fear (even, sometimes, impending doom!), the pressure to succeed that you place on your own shoulders—these are the burdens that may accompany critical events and interactions for you.

But now you're letting all of that go as you reach a state of emptiness.

You're *free.*

And so…UP you *float.*

It's easy because you're completely empty, remember? You're the Balloon Man or Balloon Lady, floating now above the heads of everyone. Breathe in and you go higher. Exhale and you float a little lower.

Imagine: you can be as light as you want just by breathing! You're released.

Float over (in your mind) to your office now, or the boardroom, or that important client's conference room, or any place that tends to bring on stress or anxiety for you. Everything certainly looks different from where you're floating above it all now, doesn't it?

Nothing whatsoever, including even high-stakes events, has any weight for the Balloon Lady or the Balloon Man.

Can you use this exercise to lighten your frame of mind just before you face your next stressful encounter?

Why not?

Exercise 32: Neutral Mask

This exercise and the next one are two visualization techniques that can help reduce your anxiety that happen to come directly from the theater. Though very different in approach, both techniques harness the power of performance to make you a more confident and focused individual. The first exercise is the Neutral Mask.

The Neutral Mask. This device is exactly what it sounds like: a human mask that displays no expression whatever. It's typically a light structure made out of leather or neoprene, secured with an elastic band that fits over the back of the wearer's head. The following is a description of the neutral mask's purpose:

The Neutral Mask doesn't have any dramatic expression, and allows the actor to explore a state of *pure presence*, in the here and now of space. With this mask the actor explores the state of neutrality that exists *before the action.* ...It lives in the present, and allows the actor to explore economy of movement (italics added).[2]

The neutral mask is a mask of complete calmness that exists only in the present. This means that the performer wearing the mask embodies tremendous potential: nothing is happening yet or is preordained; everything is possible from this point on.

Consider: by entering such a state mentally (of course, you don't actually wear a mask) if you are about to "perform" in some way—from giving a presentation to chatting with the new VP of Sales at the breakfast networking event, etc.—and you have anxiety about it, your performance can be fresh and without strain. You have gifted yourself the release of the neutral mask, where anything is possible!

For once, there is no self-fulfilling prophecy of failure waiting in the wings. The world of the "performance" you're about to give is yours to populate with new hope and promise. Wearing the neutral mask, you can truly start out in a neutral state, unburdened by anything that has gone before (from you or others).

For the purpose of this exercise, you needn't buy a neutral mask from a theatrical supply store. Simply assume as neutral an expression as you can manage. Truly: just as emotions elicit physical responses (a confused person's brow becomes furrowed, a surprised person's eyes open wide, etc.), the opposite works as well—by taking on a sad expression, you'll actually feel sadder, and so on.

Now, stand and imagine you're about to say something important to some *people* of importance. But just before you begin, slip on your invisible "neutral mask." Your facial features now show no emotion (and you're not revealing your emotions in your physical behavior either). Because your face is set in a neutral mode, you're neither thinking about the past nor anticipating anything about to happen, i.e., projecting yourself into the future: instead, *you're completely in the present.* For that reason, this moment, and you who occupy it, are in an instant of limitless potential.

What a marvelous place to be in just before you do something that you know will challenge you! From your neutral starting place, the important attributes of power, control, and dynamism can flow from you…and grow.

Exercise 33: The Actor's Box

This exercise calls for a completely different approach. Instead of inhabiting a neutral place without thought or intention, you'll be consciously thinking about matters that are likely to intrude upon your focus and awareness.

The Actor's Box is a make-believe item: a small invisible cabinet that you lock with a tiny imaginary key. Picture the cabinet as being small enough that you could carry it with you if it actually existed as a solid object. Actors use this box as a temporary home for all the personal little *demon-thoughts* that are apt to nip at them and spoil their upcoming performance.

You'll be using the box in the same way, to keep you focused throughout whatever task you've been called upon to perform. The more high-profile the job, the better it is to enlist the aid of the Actor's Box as you get ready.

Let's say your boss has asked you to give an update to the team on Project X. The idea of this exercise is for you to practice the technique you're about to learn below *just before* it's time for you to go to the conference room to deliver the update. And so you'll take your imaginary actor's box with you to get ready.

Here's what to do:

- Ten or fifteen or twenty minutes before you're about to speak, find a private quiet place. Set the imaginary box down next to you.

- Turn the little key and open the door. The box is, of course, empty at this point.

- Now spend a few moments with the things that are on your mind or bothering you today. The nature of the thoughts or worries doesn't matter. They simply need to be something that you don't want to bring "on stage" with you when you're presenting.

- *Validate* each of those worries or concerns by thinking about it for at least twenty seconds, and acknowledge it to its face. In other words, give each pressing matter a bit of attention, a little face-time. If you need to make a decision on this matter, tell yourself that you *will* make a decision…later. Once you've spent enough time validating each individual concern or worry as something that needs to be dealt with, place it in the box.

- Repeat the procedure for up to six things that you'd rather not have intruding into your thoughts as you're about to speak. These can be related to your job, or they can be family issues, health matters, upcoming deadlines, things you have to apologize for, etc., etc.

- Now swing the tiny door to your imaginary Actor's Box closed, and lock it. Put the "key" in a safe place.

- *The worries that might immediately intrude into your thoughts when you need to be otherwise focused are now safely inside your Actor's Box.* They can't reach you for the next forty-five minutes when you'll be delivering the update to your boss and her team. That was the deal you made with them in exchange for the face-time and paying attention to their "concerns."

- Since you've given each of them a little time and attention (which they were clamoring for), they'll stay quiet for the hour or two or however long it will be that you'll be participating in this event. (It's a good idea to make such a deal with them as a group before you start talking to them individually.) They'll now behave themselves for a while.

If on the other hand you had *ignored* or *repressed any of them*, one or more of them would certainly have burst into your thoughts at the moment you could least afford them to! (There's always one or two of those types in the group.) Instead, they're all now taking a nice nap and won't bother you.

BTW, if you forget to go back to the box to let them out after your presentation is over, don't worry. They're determined little critters, and they'll find their way back to you with no trouble whatsoever.

Exercise 34: The Spotlight Techniques

The two visualizations you just practiced are designed to get you into a positive state of mind prior to some kind of performance. The next two exercises, by contrast, are for calming and centering you *during* your interactions with others, whether individuals or groups.

The exercises are called "The Spotlight Techniques," and you have a choice as to which of them to practice. Of course, you can try them both. Some of our clients at The Genard Method say that the Spotlight Techniques are *the* most helpful visualizations they learned to help them overcome in-the-moment fear and stage fright. But you can judge for yourself. Whichever approaches among those introduced in this chapter work for you are the visualizations you should use.

Spotlight Technique No. 1 is meant to be a completely practical and hands-on technique, and it comes from the world of the theater. Spotlight Technique No. 2 is more spiritual in nature, and you may find that such an approach is attractive to you.

SPOTLIGHT TECHNIQUE NO. 1

When you're overly nervous and anxious, you tend to place yourself in a "third degree" spotlight. The *third degree* is the name for an intense interrogation. It's often associated with the harsh bright light police detectives used in days gone by to sweat out a confession from a suspect (while the rest of the room and the cops present there remained mysteriously in the dark). The harsh light trained on the suspect (who was always forced to sit in a hard straight-backed chair, sometimes while handcuffed to the table) was unrelenting.

A spotlight—whether it's in an interrogation room or on a stage (where it's called a "follow-spot")—is always overly bright, hard-edged, and can be physically and mentally uncomfortable. The truth is, however, you *voluntarily* train such a spotlight on yourself when you convince yourself that the people you're speaking to, or the situation itself, is unforgiving and judgmental. And the larger or more important your audience, the more that's likely to be the case.

So here's a technique to get out from under this hot spotlight that you're imagining so vividly: turn it around! Visualize swiveling the follow-spot so it's aimed at your audience instead of at you. After all, aren't you supposed to *illuminate* your listeners? And you don't want to leave them in the *dark*, do you?

There's no doubt that it's cooler and much more comfortable outside that harsh light than inside it when it's trained on you. The added benefit is that now the light is shining on your listeners—without question the most important people in the room or auditorium!

Now you can go about your business, in terms of saying what you're here to say. You can aim for the right goal, which is to *enlighten* the stakeholders, rather than fret about how exposed and vulnerable you feel!

SPOTLIGHT TECHNIQUE NO. 2

This variation is more or less completely the opposite of the first one. Rather than thinking that there's a bright spotlight beaming down on you, *imagine that a gentle light is shining from WITHIN you.* You're no longer being subjected to the third degree by a mysterious person or persons unknown. Instead—and much more importantly—YOU are the source of the light.

Your knowledge, expertise, sympathy, and goodwill glows from within you, bathing and embracing your listeners. Far from producing anxiety, this visualization should leave you feeling warm and generous to both yourself and your audience.

What a nice feeling you may produce within yourself of confidently helping others!

Exercise 35: Writing Your Fears Away

Ready for an entirely different type of visualization?

So far in this chapter, you've been sampling ways to reduce your level of anxiety by focusing *away* your fears. Now, you're going to face those fears honestly and benefit from doing so.

There's a scientific basis for such a counter-intuitive approach. It's from a recent study which demonstrated that allowing students to write about their anxiety before an important test actually reduced the "performance loss" caused by nerves. Subjects in this experiment, along with real high-school biology test-takers, were asked either to sit quietly for 10 minutes before a test, or write about their anxiety. The result? The non-writers' test scores dropped by an average of 12 percentage points, while the writers *raised* their scores by four percentage points.[3]

So that's your assignment: Sit down now, and for the next 10 minutes write out the fears and negative thinking that are plaguing you concerning, well, anything you like. Try not to conceptualize. Instead, write down your actual emotional responses and your anxiety—what you experience mentally and physically. Also avoid rationalizing or trying to make sense of your description, for fear often has no rational component.

It's possible that you might actually enjoy not trying to *fight* your anxiety for a change. You'll be welcoming it instead, sitting down with it and having a chat!

Why would such an approach work? I believe it's because the activity is akin to the Actor's Box exercise you learned about earlier. In both cases, you're giving your fears and worries some attention—a walk in the fresh air, if you will. After all the time they've spent hidden away in dark places in your mind, it must be refreshing for them to see the light of day.

And of course out in the daylight, things don't look so scary. They're *your* fears, after all—in existence only because you've given them life. Acknowledging them and coming to terms with them may help you manage their disruptive behavior. Maybe now they'll be better behaved.

So try "Writing Your Fears Away" just before you engage in an activity that causes you anxiety. If it helps you, add the exercise to your confidence toolbox.

Exercise 36: Your Command Performance Movie

Do you remember the concepts of "Worst-Case Thinking" and "awfulizing" from Chapter 6?

Here are those descriptions again:

"Worst-Case Thinking" means imagining that a truly bad outcome is going to take place despite the slimmest of evidence. And "awfulizing" is visualizing such an adverse event occurring and subconsciously preparing for it.

Doesn't it make more sense to visualize a *positive* outcome to your participation in an event?

If you have anxiety, you probably don't need to be told that you can be your own worst enemy concerning what might happen in a stressful situation. It's time to leave such unproductive behavior behind and give yourself a head start toward success.

One way to do so is by writing out what I call a *Command Performance Movie*.

A Command Performance Movie isn't a real movie shot with a camcorder. It's a scenario that you write out to help you visualize a beneficial outcome to your endeavor. As you now know, doing so should actually help predispose you toward the result you're looking for.

You'll be writing a page or two that describes the upcoming situation. Some of the details you should mention include the following:

- Your pleasure about participating in this event.
- Your accomplishment of all of your objectives.
- Your listeners'/audience's pleasure and attentiveness (including the nods and smiles you notice).
- Your success in getting people to perceive you the way you want them to.
- Your own positive impressions and feelings about the experience.

Will all of this come to pass exactly as you're writing it now? Of course not. You're not a fortune teller, after all. The point is to give yourself a positive and upbeat scenario that's *more likely* to occur if you're actively preparing for such a result.

Here's a further hint on how to make your Command Performance Movie productive and helpful: avoid dry descriptions such as, "I deliver the presentation with last month's sales figures." Well, yes, you do, but will writing that down really help you? Instead, include your emotional experiences and that of others: "I hear the boss say 'Wow!' as I show the animated slide comparing last year's sales figures with this year's." *That's* a detail that will help put you in a positive frame of mind!

Remember, your anxiety is emotionally based. Your visualization, therefore, should focus on some emotional reward from your performance.

A sample Command Performance Movie that I created is given below as an example. This happens to be about a public speaking situation. Your movie will be different, since it will be unique to your situation and goals. Also, the example below is somewhat brief since it's only meant to give you the flavor of the exercise. Your movie should go into more depth.

Make your imagined scenario as close to the actual situation as you believe it will unfold. The purpose of the exercise isn't predictive—it's to remind you of what an enjoyable emotional experience this is going to be for you.

MY COMMAND PERFORMANCE MOVIE

Today, I'm giving the keynote address at the Mega-Movers of the Universe Convention. I'm really looking forward to this occasion. This is an important group, and I've prepared extensively to give them something dynamic and interesting.

Earlier this week, I put the finishing touches on my talk. Last night I got a good night's sleep, and I had a healthy breakfast this morning. I'm feeling good! I've also allowed myself plenty of time to get to the venue, so I'm not rushed. And it's been nice to have a few minutes to meet the people coming into the hotel ballroom and introduce myself. Now I'll no longer be talking to strangers!

I'm dressed professionally, in style with good quality clothes that aren't overly flashy. The audience senses that I'm relaxed, confident, and clearly looking forward to giving my talk and sharing ideas with them.

In fact, they can see I'm really enjoying the opportunity to speak to this group. After I'm introduced, I step to the lectern, smile, and nod to the audience. I take a slow relaxed breath, and begin my conversation with my listeners.

I speak clearly and knowledgeably in an easy, confident tone. My voice is lively and engaging. As I make eye contact with audience members, I see that they're paying attention and looking interested. I stay focused on my message, which I know is coming through loud and clear. I know this material and I'm enjoying getting it across.

When I finish, everyone smiles and applauds warmly. They've clearly enjoyed my speech. As I return to my seat I overhear someone say, "Now THAT was an interesting presentation!" I know this has been a rewarding experience for them *and* me.

NOTES

1   D.T. Suzuki, Zen Buddhism, William Barrett, ed. (New York: Three Leaves Press, 2006), 3.

2   Giovanni Fusetti, "The Neutral Mask — The Silence Before the Drama," on http://www.giovannifusetti.com/public/file/lecture_neutral.pdf

3   "Writing Your Fears Away," Wall Street Journal, January 22-23, 2011. I have adopted the title of the article for this visualization exercise.

CHAPTER 8

Biofeedback for Physical Symptoms

This chapter is concerned with relieving your anxiety during your interactions with others. The focus, however, is on the *physiological* responses that accompany your fear.

Before getting to this essential approach to controlling this type of discomfort, let's review your progress up to this point and what you've learned in the book so far:

You've been introduced to the concept of "The Person You Show the World" and how it's possible to present yourself in positive rather than negative terms (Introduction). You've learned how to calm your nerves and becoming totally relaxed (Chapter 1). Gaining an awareness of your respiration cycle and relearning natural and powerful breathing was the focus of Chapter 2. Chapter 3 identified for you the parts of the brain that control fear and anxiety, and showed you how to activate the vagus nerve to turn on your parasympathetic (calming) nervous system. The "physical you" and getting to know your body—and understanding how it is a key communication tool for you—was the focus of Chapter 4. The following chapter introduced you to the valuable Focused Relaxation Exercise and showed you six meditation exercises to help you achieve mindfulness. Chapters 6 and 7 tackled the important tool of cognitive restructuring: in particular, changing from negative self-talk to positive coping statements. The latter of those chapters taught you some hands-on actor's techniques for using positive visualization.

Taking Physical Control of Your Appearances and Participation. Now it's time to work on increasing your sense of *physical control* as a participant in stressful situations. You do this by learning how to regulate your body's responses to the "fearful" event.

That is, as well armed as you now are concerning approaches to overcoming fear, you still have to deal with how your body responds when you interact with a group or get up in front of an audience. You might say that while your brain now gets it, your *body* still isn't convinced that your problematic events are safe activities.

To put this another way: however well you deal with the psychology and emotional aspects of fear, anxiety, and lack of confidence, you can't *think* your way through your body's responses! The way to deal with what's happening to you physically is to turn those responses to your advantage. That's what we'll be looking at in this chapter.

GETTING YOURSELF READY FOR ACTION

Whatever else dealing with other people and proving yourself professionally represents for you, they are exciting activities. Among other responses, your body becomes energized and ready for action. Your job then becomes to *harness* that energy into constructive channels. Basically, you want to be relaxed yet dynamic, rather than at the mercy of undirected and even chaotic impulses.

To do so, you first need to gain a greater awareness of what's going on in terms of your physical reaction. Then you can learn how to use *biofeedback* to monitor your progress. By succeeding in these twin goals, you will:

- Slow down and quiet your stress response.

- Create a distraction trigger to center and calm you physically before performing.

- "Close the gate" through which stressful stimuli reach your awareness.

- Increase helpful blood flow during times of stress.

- Open your "emotional gate" for a positive performance that reliably connects with stakeholders every time, thereby gaining greater self-confidence.

THE PHYSIOLOGY OF SPEAKING FEAR

Let's take a look at how the human body responds to performance-based anxiety. This makes sense because your appearances will so often involve participating in meetings, contributing remarks, making pitches and/or providing updates, perhaps speaking to committees or panels, and most likely delivering presentations.

Going Beyond Butterflies. Many people—perhaps most— experience "butterflies" in the stomach before appearing in an important event. But to those with issues of anxiety, fear, and negative thinking, the event invokes a pressing inner need to fight the "threat" or to flee the danger: the well-known "fight-or-flight response". Since neither of those actions is possible when, say, you're giving a presentation, the mismatch between your overpowering physical reaction and the (benign) event can make you not only anxious, but confused and distracted. And of course, there are the extreme physical responses you're going through due to stress hormones that are urging you to *do* something about the danger, which isn't there in the first place!

You probably recognize some or many of these physical symptoms that you begin to experience at this point:

- Rapid, shallow breathing
- Increased heart rate
- Rise in blood pressure
- Release of the stress hormone epinephrine (also known as adrenaline)
- Release of cortisol (another, less well known stress hormone. See below.)
- Sweating
- Dry mouth
- Cold extremities, as blood retreats to vital organs and blood vessels constrict
- Cessation of digestion, peristalsis (movement of food through the bowels), and the need for elimination.

In addition, you can experience any of these common physical reactions as well:

- Pounding heart
- Dry mouth
- Becoming pale or flushed

- Shaky voice
- Trembling hands or legs
- Loss of hearing
- Tunnel vision or a mysterious "not being able to see the audience"
- Mind becoming "cobwebby" or in a fog

Obviously, fear and the sense of being in danger produces a cascade of physical symptoms. Going through any or all of this is guaranteed to affect your state of mind and ability to perform, just when you're trying to come across at your best!

This tendency of your body to respond so strongly to anxiety is the reason why the mind-based approach we've looked at so far—including cognitive restructuring, positive visualization, and increased focus and presence—isn't enough. You must control your pronounced *physical responses* as well in order to be effective in the speaking situation.[1]

THE DANGERS OF CORTISOL

One of those physical responses is the release of the stress hormone *cortisol*. Cortisol is a naturally occurring hormone produced by the adrenal glands. The beneficial effects of this substance include the following functions:

- Processing of glucose level in the body
- Regulating blood pressure
- Production of insulin to control blood sugar
- A healthy immune system
- Controlling inflammation

Certainly, these are important and beneficial physiological functions. However, it has been demonstrated that *prolonged high levels of stress-related cortisol* in the bloodstream have harmful effects on the body. For instance, if you love your job except for having to speak in public (as more than one of my clients has said), you can experience a *continuous stress response* on a weekly or even daily basis, causing cortisol to be released much too frequently.

At that point, you're susceptible to the negative effects listed below. (After all, situations in our evolution where we truly faced a danger big enough to have to fight or flee must have been fairly rare!)

- Decreased cognitive abilities
- Suppression of thyroid function
- High blood sugar
- Impairment of bone density
- Reduction in muscle tissue
- Increased blood pressure
- Reduced immune system function and response to inflammation
- Abdominal fat deposits, which are associated with health problems such as heart attack and strokes[2]

Clearly, using biofeedback to counter such a too-common extreme stress response is important to your physical well-being. To examine how to do so, let's start at the very source of the physiologically-based response to appearing in public: your awareness that you have to give a performance of some kind. Aside from your brain, there's one organ in particular that responds immediately and strongly to that news.

THE HEART OF THE MATTER

You may or may not believe that the heart is the seat of the emotions. But there's no denying that this organ plays a starring role in everyone's response to stage fright and an awareness of how our body reacts when you speak in public.

It may interest you to know, for instance, that people who fear public speaking have higher heart rates than individuals with generalized social anxiety disorder.[3] Literally, then, public speaking fear is not only "in your head."

When your pulse rate begins to gallop; when your heart pounds so that it feels like it's going to break out of your chest; when the engine of your circulatory system is startled out of its normal rhythm—you can't escape the fact that the situation is out of your control. You want to establish equilibrium again quickly. In fact, you desperately need to do so if you're going to present a calm, confident, and professional demeanor.

This, therefore, is where you need to start in terms of biofeedback—calming your heart so the rest of your body and your mind can follow.

Exercise 37: Calming the Heart

This exercise will help you determine your own "normal state" in terms of being relaxed and calm and therefore focused. Once you recognize that state, you can reliably come back to it in times of stress.

To start, first get a resting pulse. That's the number of heart beats per minute you experience when you're not overly stressed or physically exerting yourself. Take your pulse rate for ten seconds and multiply by six; or continue taking your pulse for a full minute. Make a mental note of that number. Now continue feeling your pulse as you...

...take a DEEP breath and hold it for a slow count of five. Then release that big breath all at once: *WHOOSH!*

Did you just notice any change in your pulse rate?

It's likely that you felt your heart *slow down* just after you whooshed out the breath. Why? When you inhale deeply, your heart receives a generous supply of the oxygen-rich blood it needs to pumps out to all the cells in your body. So it suddenly doesn't have to work as hard. It can, and does, relax. That's what just happened.

For you as for everyone, oxygen means life; so when your heart is fully oxygenated, it can slow down. The other important effect produced here, is that the *controlled slowness* of the breathing process (taking the time for a deep breath) counteracts the rapid heartbeat that's characteristic of the fear response. In a sense, you just gave your heart permission to take it easy. And it did.

This physiological response is important for you to recognize and *practice*. By inducing your heart to relax and slow down, you're countering two of the most noticeable and worrying effects of anxiety: a loss of control over the situation, and the sensation that your body is working against you.

The Value of Calming Your Heart. The Calming the Heart exercise helps you reestablish control over the situation, and to create a positive physiological response to whatever is causing your stress. It also helps link your breathing to your heart rate, demonstrating that control of this connection is possible.

Practice it some more now. Once again: monitor your resting

pulse rate, breathe deeply, then exhale strongly all at once. Now you can clearly feel the link between your breathing and your physical response! The more you can use slow controlled breathing in anxiety-inducing situations, the more you'll be able to calm yourself and handle those events.

Nicely done! You've just started using biofeedback to help reduce your stress response.

Exercise 38: Calming the Nervous System

Let's take the next step: going from calming your heart in its distress to *slowing down your entire nervous system response*. That's the logical next stage in using biofeedback to control your nerves and anxiety.

If that sounds like a huge task, it isn't. Actually, it couldn't be easier. In fact, we're going to get all the help we need from a friend we met earlier in the book: your vagus nerve.

Do you remember Chapter 3, which was concerned with the neurology of fear and anxiety? Here is some information from that chapter.

> The PARASYMPATHETIC NERVOUS SYSTEM (the "rest and digest system") *is the one that calms you down.* The SYMPATHETIC NERVOUS SYSTEM ("fight-or-flight)" on the other hand, does the opposite by spurring you to quick and decisive action in times of emergency. Obviously, it's the former and not the latter response we want to help calm you and keep your nerves quiet.

You probably also recall that *the vagus nerve is responsible for slowing down your heart rate with each exhalation.* The helpfulness of that information is immediately obvious, isn't it? — When it comes to turning on your nervous system's calming response, then, you do it through using the action of breathing focused on the vagus nerve!

Do you remember the 4-4-6-2 breathing pattern from that chapter as well? That's the pattern that has you inhale for a count of four, pause for the same count, exhale for a count of six, then stop the process for a count of two (and then repeat).

Since the vagus nerve *always* slows your heart when you exhale, by making your exhalation deliberately longer, you are increasing your ability to rein in your galloping heart (since the vagus nerve's slowing action becomes stronger). In this way, you enlist *your whole nervous system* to help you counter anxiety, not just create a slower heart rate as happened when you whooshed out your breath (Exercise 37, above).

Since you know how to do it, practice the 4-4-6-2 pattern now. It's another valuable way to add a biofeedback mechanism to help you counter your pronounced physical response. And like all good biofeedback, you can feel its benefits immediately.

Exercise 39: Closing the Stress Gate

You've just learned something concerning how the mind-to-body channel works in terms of you perceiving and responding to stress. You may have heard of this process compared to a gate, especially with regard to controlling pain. Visualizing keeping the gate closed, for instance, can diminish the amplitude of pain signals—or at least one's focus on them—that reach the consciousness.

Methods of "closing" the gate include simply being distracted; relaxation exercises; meditation; and intense focus on a task. In times of emergency or danger, such as in a battle or car accident, people have performed amazing feats despite injuries that should have been accompanied by intense pain (or in fact have been impossible to achieve). Incredibly, they report that in these moments of crisis they were unaware of any pain.[4]

Learning that it's possible to control pain or manage an excessive physical response to stress is enormously useful in terms of reducing anxiety and letting go of fears. In Chapter 6 of this book ("Changing Your Negative Thinking"), you practiced reshaping your cognitive responses to fear and anxiety. Now you can work on a closely related area: the physiological changes that take place based on your thinking and emotional response. In Exercise 37, above, that process involved calming the heart through a simple breathing technique. In this exercise, "Closing the Stress Gate," you'll visualize disrupting the messages from your body to your brain that keep reminding you of your fear. In effect, you'll be closing the gate to an unproductive part of your consciousness.

What Closes Your Gate? The important question is: What closes the gate for *you*? If you already have an effective distraction,[5] a relaxation exercise, a meditation technique, or other trigger that works by drawing your attention or redirecting your attention, you may already know how to effectively close the gate. If not, I would like to offer a visualization that may work for you:

FOCUS ON MAKING THE VARIOUS AREAS IN YOUR AWARENESS A SINGLE AREA.

That is, close the gate to the noisy mob of distractions that is trying to bully its way into your consciousness. The fact is, there are almost always too many things pulling your focus away from where it needs to be. You're therefore forced into the role of *multitasking*. Multitasking is a completely counterproductive habit in professional endeavors because 100% of your focus needs to be on a single outcome in complicated business scenarios. Some of the tasks you're attending to (and shouldn't be) involve the care and feeding of your anxiety, and so you should certainly stop doing that one. Besides, it's a precarious situation to have four or five balls in the air at any one time in front of stakeholders. No wonder your fears and inadequacies are crowding out productive thoughts in your mind!

Let all of these things go—let all of the balls fall to the ground and bounce off the stage...who cares? Instead, allow yourself the luxury of focusing on the *one area* that truly matters to you at this moment, whatever you're talking about or reacting to:

Your listeners and the message you have to get across to them. That's *always* the target you should be aiming for.

THE CLOSING THE STRESS GATE VISUALIZATION

Now, the visualization itself:

- As you prepare to speak, in your mind see yourself stepping through an actual gate. Now immediately latch the gate behind you (before that crowd of worries can scurry inside).

- The gate is now officially closed behind you. Nothing at all in terms of fears, anxieties, worries, or negative thoughts can get in.

- In *front* of you, on the other hand (on your side of the gate), are the people you're here to talk to. You and they are the only ones in the room or auditorium. It's peaceful and cozy in here, and you and your listeners are here because of a mutual interest in the topic. What a nice situation!

- Outside the gate, the winds of discord may be blowing. There may even be a gale going on, reflecting the chaotic nature of all those negative thoughts and fears that you successfully shut out.

- But from where you stand or sit, the sound is far away and you can no longer really hear it.

Exercise 40: Opening the Emotional Gate

As important as it is to close the gate against fear-induced thinking that will alter your behavior, it's vital to *open* the emotional barrier you've erected against your listeners. ...Oh, yes, you have!

You may not realize you've been doing this, but it's still true. Why? Well, obviously, if you have speaking fear or social anxiety, you've decided somewhere along the line that a group of people waiting for you to perform is a dangerous thing. Without them demanding that you prove yourself like this, why would there be a problem?

What this means in terms of your performance is that in order to gain protection, you start to subtly (or more overtly) hide your true self from their view. But to fully overcome the negative physical responses that you're experiencing—to feel unburdened and physically free—you have to emerge from this fine and private hiding place.

That's because an "emotional gate" that's latched shut sends your body the wrong signals as to how it should respond. Remember, your emotional make-up and your physiological responses are closely linked. Appropriate emotions for speaking in public include joy, fun, and an eagerness to share what you know—not dread, aversion, and a grim determination to survive the torture that's about to occur. Think of the *nonverbal cues* you're exhibiting when you experience the latter set of emotions!

As I've said many times, some nervousness about appearing in public is normal and healthy; anxiety is not. If you retreat emotionally from your audience, it will only prolong the pain and leave you more vulnerable. Naturally, you'll be less confident, and as a result, less successful.

So at this point I want to talk about opening the emotional gate so you can be both strong *and* vulnerable for your audience. People who show their vulnerability make audiences want to reach out to them. Those who wear armor or bare their teeth at listeners send them in the opposite direction.

Learning to Accept Your Environment. Consider the shiver response. It's normal to shiver when you're cold, because your body is trying to generate heat through movement in the muscles. Eventually, though, constant shivering just reminds you that you're cold, and the cycle keeps repeating. But I discovered during the Massachusetts winters when I was growing up that if I consciously *stopped* the shivering—if I willed myself to remain still—I didn't feel as cold! In a way, I was acknowledging the low temperatures and telling myself to just remain calm in the face of them.

In other words, *I was accepting my environment rather than trying to escape from it.* Can you see how doing the same thing in front of an audience will keep you calm and physically poised, rather than tightening up and "shivering" with dread?

Acupuncture provides another example. Acupuncturists believe that the body's energy or *qi* (pronounced "chee") is being blocked in places. The acupuncture needles penetrate these blockages, helping release your body's energy along the "meridians" through which the qi flows. Once your qi is flowing freely again, pain and other negative effects of blocked energy are lessened.

When Emotions Are Blocked, Sharing Can't Take Place. Frightened and anxious people often block their emotions in a similar fashion when they appear in front of others. The essential interaction between speaker and audience—the organic "back and forth of ideas and emotions" can't then take place. How could they, when one side (the speaker) is blocking the signal?

To be in the spotlight in front of a group when this is happening—when no emotion-based communication is taking place between you and them—is to virtually guarantee that you'll be miserable on stage. And if you feel unhappy, you will reflect it (and show it) physically. That's the negative biofeedback loop that ties emotional unhappiness to physical discomfort in public speaking.

Why is this important? Because emotions matter more in professional settings than we allow ourselves to admit. Audiences won't remember the facts and figures you throw at them as much as they will recall how you made them *feel*. Of course, the process also works in the opposite direction: you will remember particular audiences and events by your emotional response to them—and theirs to you—more strongly than, say, the questions they asked. And then there's the little matter of emotions being part of *every* decision we make, including business decisions. (I explain this further in Exercise 74, "Storytelling To Create An Emotional Response.")

Avoiding "Excellence". But this is only part of your unhappiness as someone who is anxious when interacting with others. Some of it also comes from your desire to be "excellent." In fact, one of the greatest fallacies of performing well in your professional role is that you may think you have to be an excellent public speaker. The truth is you only have to be an *honest* speaker. If you know what you're talking about and are passionate about sharing it with others, you will come across as natural and interesting. And if you don't have the necessary knowledge, expertise, or genuine concern for your listeners (or haven't prepared adequately), trying to "be excellent" simply won't work.

The surest path to excellence when dealing with others is not to aim for the ideal of perfection but for honesty. Audiences want to hear *you*, not you-trying-to-be-better-than-you-really-are.

When you get used to that idea—when you can stand in front of a group of people honestly and give them only what you're capable of—you'll be taking a huge weight off your shoulders. After all, what's easier: being you, or being excellent?

When you speak as yourself rather than as an ideal, something infinitely valuable will emerge: true communication. Open the emotional gate and welcome your audience in—in other words, let them see your vulnerability rather than being terrified of it. Your confidence will benefit enormously.

Exercise 41: Facial Relaxation

It's a genuine not-seeing-the-forest-for-the-trees situation. — Your *face* is helping generate your own negative biofeedback.

Facial expressiveness or countenance is an area many people ignore when thinking about nonverbal communication. Yet your face is not only highly flexible, it's an essential tool for getting your message and meaning across, especially in terms of subtly and nuance.

Consider for a moment how visually dependent our species is on the human face. Facial structures and features allow us to recognize one person from another. (We don't depend upon smell, as many animals do.) Equally significantly, we interpret intention and meaning by the finely tuned expressions we see on another person's face. Obviously, if you're a stone-faced communicator, you're putting yourself and your audience at a disadvantage!

Because the face is physical and therefore one of your nonverbal communication tools, it can become tight and unresponsive when you're stressed. It's made up of muscles, after all. A common place for holding tension, for instance, is the area around the eyes as well as the *look in your eyes themselves.*

Clearly, it's helpful for you to practice relaxing your facial muscles so they can remain pliant enough for full expressiveness. Knowing that you're communicating using all the tools available to you should give you confidence! Along those lines, try this facial relaxation exercise (I'd wait until your boss is not around):

- Allow your face to go completely slack. You might not want to look in a mirror while doing this, as your muscle tone will not be especially flattering. Pay particular attention to your eye sockets. Feel the tension you hold in this "secret" spot. Now let it melt away.

- You should be experiencing a feeling of calmness and a sense of being in the present moment, akin to the Neutral

Mask exercise. Now tighten your face—not radically, but just enough so that you can sense how you may habitually exhibit some facial tension without even realizing it.[6] Imagine how that tension can incrementally drain your energy all day long.

- Go completely slack again, and hold that facial posture. *Now slowly allow your personality to flow back into your features.* This is you at your best: the image of calm attentiveness, without any tension.

- Use your muscle memory to retain how your face feels when it's like this: alive with your personality, minus tension. It's one more biofeedback channel through which you can send yourself messages that get you to the right place physically. And you'll be helping to keep those wrinkles away too!

Exercise 42: The Healing Breath

The Healing Breath is an original approach we use at The Genard Method. It's a way to help liberate yourself from negative feelings while relaxing your nervous system through inward-directed breathing and awareness.

Remember in Chapter 5 when you practiced the Focused Relaxation exercise? You became aware of thoughts that arose in your mind—but importantly, *you didn't indulge those thoughts.* You noticed them but did not engage them; nor did you actively resist them—you simply noticed them and let them continue on their way. In a similar fashion, The Healing Breath helps you recognize unhelpful emotions without perpetuating them. By practicing The Healing Breath, you allow your body to respond physically to healthy breathing, so the signals you receive are positive and affirming. Here's how to do so:

1. Sit quietly, relaxing your facial muscles and your eyes as in the previous exercise. Allow any negative energy to become heavy and sink downward, like sediment in a pond. Don't disturb this energy, just let it settle down and be still.

2. Now with your eyes closed, *visualize* yourself smiling. Don't actually smile, however; just visualize yourself doing it. First, your face will relax...and then, without consciously activating the muscles, you'll genuinely smile. (Smiles are infectious, even to ourselves!) Remember that a smile begins at the corner of the eyes, not at the mouth.

3. While still smiling (it's probably a gentle smile), consciously follow your breath. Both your smile and your breathing should feel easy and delicious. If your face feels in any way tight from smiling, change the smile to a grin, and keep it going. (A grin can make the "crinkly" feeling at the corner of your eyes even more noticeable.)

4. Scan yourself inwardly. ...Any anger present? Any impatience or frustration? Any fear? Anxiety? Lack of confidence? If so, turn your "smile-breath" on each of these emotions until the negative energy residing there melts, sinking downward in that pond.

5. Now expand your breathing, letting it reach every nook and cranny in your body. *Send* your breath everywhere, into every space and organ of your physical presence. *Your breath is the healing solution.* Allow it to get inside you and fill you everywhere.

NOTES

1 One chapter of The Confidence Book has already covered, in part, an area based in physiological response: Chapter 2: 'To Know Life in Every Breath': Breathing Techniques.

2 http://stress.about.com/od/stresshealth/a/cortisol.htm.

3 Hoffmann and Otto, 10.

4 "Use the Gate Control Model to Manage Pain," handout from Brigham and Women's Hospital Pain Management Center.

5 One of our clients, a nurse, particularly liked the idea of a distraction to take her mind off her fear just before she spoke in public. She understood perfectly how this would help her, since she'd already been using the technique for years with patients who feared needles: she would say something to distract them just before she inserted the needle in their arm.

6 Speaking of "infectious" facial movements: Did you know that dogs will yawn as easily as we do when they see a yawn...and that they'll yawn much more easily when their owner yawns? It's true!

CHAPTER 9

Dealing With Panic Attacks

This chapter discusses three ways you can help yourself if you experience a panic attack during an event, presentation, interview, meeting, etc. In it, I'll be sharing three "escape hatches" you can use if one of these situations becomes unbearably uncomfortable and distressing for you.

You may need one of these escape hatches someday. That would be if, despite your best intentions and even after learning the techniques in this book, you feel a powerful and overwhelming need to flee the situation. You can guess that apart from the embarrassment involved, that's not the best career move you can make.

The suggestions you'll find elsewhere in books and articles about what to do when you feel a panic attack coming on are, to put it mildly, lacking in knowledge and substance. Here are some actual strategies offered by "experts" and lay persons for dealing with public speaking-induced panic attacks:

- Speak to people's foreheads.
- Look at specific points in the room and talk to those areas.

- Take deep breaths before speaking.
- Pray.
- Talk to someone about it.
- Remember that it is a curable condition.
- Contact a medical professional and seek guidance.
- Realize you didn't die from the attack [then you'll be able to laugh about it!].
- Build your confidence back to where it used to be.
- Don't fear fear.
- React with confidence at the instant you feel the anxiety attack.
- Push your energy outward, not back into your body.
- Practice.
- Take a tranquilizer.
- Tell yourself you can do this, so *stop panicking!*
- Accept the fact that public speaking is not inherently stressful.
- Relinquish your need to control your environment.
- Eat foods with life in them (Where, I wonder, are these miraculous foods found?)
- Distract yourself.
- Eliminate anxious thoughts.

And the perennial favorite:
- Imagine the audience naked or in their underwear.

Can you figure out how any of these techniques will stop a panic attack in its tracks? I certainly can't!

Look at those approaches again. You'll notice that not a single one discusses the essential task of the speaker suffering a panic attack, i.e., the need to deal with the situation that's actually taking place!

The three solutions I offer below ("Escape Hatches #1, #2, and #3") all work by doing just that: allowing you to face the situation and handle it rather than giving in to the panic. That is, they place you securely in the environment you're actually a part of and realistically help you deal productively *and immediately* with the situation at hand.

I've created these approaches because I believe that public speaking-related panic attacks (and the same can be said of other situations where you will be speaking or participating in some other way) *always* arise from the same cause: a speaker who feels divorced from his or her audience. The audience may be viewed as hostile, bored, uncaring, or judgmental, or sometimes, just too large. But in every instance, the speaker feels that the audience is *out there,* and he or she is *up here,* across a physical and psychological divide. And "here"—with you facing a dozen, 50, or 500 stakeholders—always seems like a lonely and dangerous place. No wonder, then, that you may feel like Jonathan Harker, the young man kept against his will in the novel *Dracula* who despairs when he realizes he's a prisoner in the count's castle and says to himself: "There is no escape for me!"

What Not to Do During a Panic Attack. In fact, the harsh truth is that there *is* no quick-and-easy solution when a panic attack hits you during an appearance—or at least one that won't be noticed by everyone. You can't run screaming from the room (unless you don't actually enjoy your job any more). And you can't stop the presses and say, "Sorry everybody, I simply can't go on." Just as in life, the only way out is *through*—and the time to deal with the situation is "now."

How to Stop a Panic Attack. To stop a panic attack, you must eliminate the cause of the panic. As I say above, that is often the feeling that you're divorced from the audience or group of stakeholders and you're well aware that you're failing publicly (for instance, you're making a pitch to a prospective client or team that you can feel is going disastrously).

What needs to happen at that moment is that you need to step off the merry-go-round of your negative and completely unproductive thoughts, and bring yourself back to the here-and-now. *That's* what matters (and that's what is really taking place, not wherever your negative thinking is leading you). In other words, embrace the reality. That reality is almost certainly the fact that you're interacting with people concerning a topic that's of mutual interest to all of you. You're sharing with your listeners something valuable and irreplaceable that's unfolding in *this* moment and in *this* place, not on Planet Doom.

And that realization should be an invitation to excitement and confidence in your thoughts, not fear.

So, with that in mind, below are the three escape hatches available to you.

Exercise 43: Escape Hatch #1: The Only Way Out Is Through

In this first "escape hatch" strategy, follow these five steps when you're starting to panic, in exactly this sequence:

1. STOP whatever it is you are saying, doing, or thinking.

2. Breathe deeply, once.

3. Bring yourself back into mindfulness. You do this by simply inhabiting the present moment again. That means embracing it fully, without being—or wishing you were—someplace else. (You can refresh your memory of doing this through the Mini-Vacation exercise in Chapter 7, when you switched your sensory awareness between two locations.)

4. *Look* at the people there with you.

5. Resume talking about whatever it is that matters to *them*, NOT you. If you weren't doing that before, do it now!

If you're concerned that the moment when you stop and take a deep breath will be too noticeable, use body language to make it look as if you're gathering your thoughts. Or take a drink of water after you breathe deeply. Use your wits!

Giving Yourself to Others Is Liberating. The key to this escape hatch is that, when you give yourself over to the needs of others, your self-consciousness about yourself disappears. Notice that Step 5 says, "Talk about what matters to *them*." As soon as you do, you'll realize that you're in the right place, with the right listeners, discussing something that you're mutually interested in. After all, whatever you're sharing with them is almost certainly not about you and your moment of fear—it's about what you need to tell them and what they need to hear. Clearly, if you are doing so, you belong here with them, not somewhere else!

It's all a reminder that in the end, dealing with reality is so much easier and more productive than running away from it.

And also, that honesty and authenticity trump showman-ship every time, lending you real confidence, not the showy but empty kind.

Exercise 44: Escape Hatch #2: Movement Will Set You Free

Have you heard of the theory of EMBODIED COGNITION? It states that we think not only with our brain, but also with our body. If you consider this for a moment, it makes perfect sense. Haven't you paced back and forth while trying to remember something? Don't ideas pop into your head sometimes when you're driving or taking a shower? When you're scribbling notes for an idea, don't you often think of something *else* you should be writing down? And doesn't taking a walk usually clear your head and realign your thinking?

The common element in each of these examples is *movement*. Embodied cognition goes even further, theorizing that *we can actually use movement to help us think better*.

In fact, experiments have demonstrated this benefit. As a recent newspaper article reported:

> A series of studies…[showed] that children can solve math problems better if they are told to use their hands while thinking. Another recent study suggested that stage actors remember their lines better when they are moving. And in one study published last year, subjects asked to move their eyes in a specific pattern while puzzling through a brainteaser were twice as likely to solve it.[1]

It stands to reason, then, that movement can help you think

at one of the moments when you desperately need to do so: during a public speaking panic attack. So if you find yourself in the speaking pressure-cooker and your agitation is building, and you're feeling overwhelmed and you're sure you won't remember what to say next...

Move!

Cross the room to point to something on the slide screen. Visit a section of the audience you haven't been to in a while. Step back to the lectern if you've been standing somewhere else on the stage, or move away from it if you've been stuck behind the thing for some time. Take a few steps toward another part of the room as you make your next point. It doesn't really matter what you do, just move!

Embodied cognition is telling you that simply by moving, you'll break up the logjam, *think* more clearly, and help bring yourself out of the panic. Moving in any way will also help you feel less trapped. Also, the nervous energy building in your muscles from adrenaline needs a release, and movement will help provide it.

So use the outlet of movement before you overload.

Exercise 45: Escape Hatch #3: Inhabiting Your Body

As I mentioned earlier in this chapter, a primary cause of a spiraling panic attack is the desire to escape the presence of your audience. In a sense, you want to be anywhere but here, dealing with the present situation. But you *must* deal with it! Longing to be anywhere else in the universe may be momentarily comforting, but it keeps you worlds away from being present and engaged with your listeners.

When your mind is seducing you into panic like this, it's time to get physical.

By all means, stay engaged with your audience. But now start paying attention to your body.

First, *ground* yourself: feel the soles of your feet on the floor, and the firm foundation standing like that gives you. Imagine you have roots that go down into the earth, reaching deep and wide so you're steadfast and secure.

Second, feel your breath *energize* you. Imagine that your breathing is *electric*. When you inhale, you're a cylinder of pure power, lit up like a neon sign!

Third, become aware of the physical sensations inside you: Where is the tension? the energy flow? the power? the heat? — The miracle of life is running through you, giving you strength and animating you. To notice what's going on in your body is to be completely present, to absolutely occupy the here-and-now.

Becoming aware of your body in this way—inhabiting it while you still remain present for others and even while speaking—is a potent antidote to the fear-induced need to escape your circumstances. You don't need a place of refuge at this moment. You're right where you need to be, mentally, yes, but also as a body that's occupying an enjoyable moment in time.

As I said earlier in the book, nothing brings you back to the present like focusing on your breath and how it is animating (and centering) your body.

NOTES

1   Drake Bennett, "Don't Just Stand There, Think," Boston Globe, January 13, 2008.

CHAPTER 10

Body Language and Nonverbal Communication

You want to *move* your listeners, don't you? That means you have to move!

Like an actor in rehearsal trying to connect with the *action* of the play, you should literally move to help create a visual component to the forward momentum of your ideas. Your body is one of your primary means of communication; and if you don't employ it, you diminish the strength and impact of your remarks. You also make it more difficult for *yourself* to show what you feel. As team members, video conference participants, prospective customers, and audiences, we're depending upon that visual demonstration to know that you're committed and passionate about what you believe.

ARE YOU INTERESTING TO WATCH?

Do you know why some salespeople keep a mirror by their telephone at work? It's because they know that their facial expressions can be "heard" on the other end of the line. These people are often taught to smile before they pick up the receiver (or click the "Answer" prompt on their cell phone), so that they will *sound friendly* when they say hello. It's just one example of how what you do physically is reflected in people's responses to you.

When I'm working with a client on using body language, I often suggest that they practice in front of a mirror. I tell them to give their talk exactly as they will when it's time to perform the speech—including forming all the words—but without vocalizing. In another words, they should *look* exactly as they will in performance, including movement, gestures, and facial expressions, though it will all be delivered in silence. Then, I suggest, they should ask themselves some questions:

- "Am I an interesting speaker to watch, even if my listeners weren't able to hear the words I'm saying?[1]

- "Am I an animated presence…or am I too static?"

- "Can people tell how I feel about this just by looking at me?"

- "Do I display any passion for my topic?"

- "Do I look like I'm reaching out to the audience so they'll understand me?"

All of these questions touch upon including a *physical dimension* to your public speaking. Audiences depend upon your eye contact, facial expressions, gestures, stance, posture, movement on stage, and generally, a "reaching out" to them through your efforts to get closer to them (such as moving to the downstage edge of a stage) and the inclusive body language you display. You should never plan out how you will respond physically at any moment to the audience in attendance. But you should also be aware that you *have* a physical presence and not just get up there and deliver information like a robot speaking.

Speaking to groups large and small are actually opportunities to connect with others who share your passion (or at least your interest) in a subject. And the physical components involved—including such things as your nonverbal expressiveness, the audience's presence at the venue, and the shape and size and "feel" of the space itself—are indisputable elements of the transaction.

JUST HOW IMPORTANT IS BODY LANGUAGE?

We're told that nonverbal behaviors constitute 60 to 65 percent of interpersonal communication.[2] Another famous study claimed that the number can be as high as 93 percent, at least when discussing feelings or attitudes.[3] And one well-known researcher claims that at least 90 percent of emotional messages are nonverbal.[4]

With numbers like these, it's hard to dispute that a strong undercurrent of emotional responses to you and what you *show* audiences occurs when you speak. In other words, a large part of your influence depends upon what you are showing, not just what you're saying. It's the old idea that "it isn't what you say, but how you say it." Among the tools for speaking in this way include vocal dynamics, which I discuss in the next chapter. But just as powerfully, it also means your ability to incorporate *physical expressiveness*. It's all part of expressing what you feel!

You can see this in action in one of the most popular TED Talks: Jill Bolte Taylor's "My Stroke of Insight." The title of the talk is a clever play on words because Dr. Taylor—herself a brain scientist—suffered a massive stroke in 1996 at the age of 37, requiring an eight-year recovery.[5] Dr. Taylor's talk is fascinating because of her unique viewpoint and experience. That is, she both *experienced* and *observed* the deterioration of her brain's language and cognitive abilities over a four-hour period after a blood vessel "exploded."

Apart from her remarkable recovery—demonstrated by her incisive and fascinating speech—her TED Talk is a lesson in how to translate one's spoken content into the physical expression of that material. Dr. Taylor is particularly good at using her arms and hands expansively in a way that reflects the size and scope of her topic. If you watch the talk, you'll also notice how she moves within the tight red circle (the hallmark of TED Talks), while pivoting regularly to display her upper body to every part of the audience. Here's a speaker who understands the need to move while speaking on the public stage!

Speakers who move are certainly more interesting to watch than those who are "talking heads." But learning to use body language while speaking actually involves a more fundamental issue. It's this: physical expression—along with other forms of nonverbal communication—has the power to transcend cognitive thinking. For one thing, it's capable of producing a *gestalt*, or wholesale comprehension of a concept without a complex thinking process leading to a conclusion. Such forms of expression can be very powerful, even explosive. They can be greatly aided through a speech that's literally *embodied* by the speaker.

So pay attention to the care and feeding of the physical aspects of your speaking persona. If you haven't ever thought that you need to express yourself physically as well as intellectually in a presentation, I hope this chapter convinces you. As modern dance pioneer Martha Graham put it: "The body says what words cannot."[6]

Once again, then, the question: how important is body language? In law enforcement, appropriate body language can be a matter of life or death. In an FBI study of criminals who had attacked police officers, the prisoners revealed that they scoped out how easy a target an officer would be based on such factors as sloppy or neat dress, and how he or she carried themselves. [Note: Vague and imprecise language when dealing with suspects was also considered.] The conclusion? — In approaching a subject, "poor vocal tone and body language could get you killed."[7]

Exercise 46: Are You Revealing More Than You Want To?

Don't look now—but someone may be reading your mind.

Actually, you should be looking, and paying attention to what you're seeing. Reading someone's nonverbal communication can give you important clues about what that person is thinking and feeling about you. Of course, the same applies in the opposite direction. You might, for instance, be displaying a lack of confidence through the nonverbal signals you're sending out to others. And if you are, many of the people watching you will pick up on it.

It would be a shame, of course, if, after all the work you've been doing to buttress your confidence, you realize that you were actually giving signals indicating a lack of confidence. And that would translate into others having little confidence in you!

Here are 10 ways your body language may be giving the game away in this fashion.

BE CAREFUL OF WHAT YOU'RE REVEALING!

1. **Saying one thing but showing another.** Recently my family and I were having lunch at a restaurant in New Hampshire, and I asked the hostess for directions to a bike touring company where we had reservations for an afternoon ride. She said: "Go out of the restaurant to the end of the block, then take a left," while indicating a *right* turn with her right hand. I asked whether I should follow her words or her gesture. She laughed, realizing what she had done. The reason? Probably just a momentary lack of attentiveness. (She really did mean *right*, which is another indication that nonverbal communication or what you *show* usually trumps what you say.) If that happens in everyday situations (and you know it does), imagine how speaking in public can make you or your audience feel distracted. Stay focused!

2. **The "giveaway gesture."** Like micro-expressions (emotion-based facial poses that are often too fleeting to be noticed consciously by the other person), we can make bodily gestures that betray our true feelings despite what we're saying. When broadcast journalist Diane Sawyer asked Amanda Knox in a televised interview if she'd been present during her roommate's murder in Italy, Ms. Knox answered "No," then immediately and emphatically nodded "*Yes.*" Which of the conflicting signals would you believe? (As I say above, generally people will trust a physical display over verbal content.)

3. **The vocal disconnect.** A recent article stated that financial analysts now pay close attention to the vocal patterns of public company CEOs they are interviewing on quarterly earnings calls. If an executive paints a rosy scenario for, say, a stock's future performance, while at the same time *sounding* pessimistic, the analysts may not believe him or her. As with movement and gestures, listeners will trust vocal rather than verbal input, since the voice is also a tool of nonverbal communication. 'Nuff *said.*

4. **"Leaving" listeners while you're thinking.** This one is a little more subtle—until you start to notice it. You'll see speakers who, in the middle of remarks, look up at the ceiling while they're thinking. Sometimes, it's off to the side or at the floor. (This is hugely noticeable in television or visual podcasts, where the camera is usually tightly focused on the interviewee's face.) Whenever a speaker's gaze leaves the audience he or she is talking to, listeners have a right to think, "Hey, I'm over here!"

SO, A GENERAL RULE YOU SHOULD REMEMBER: *If you're not looking at your audience, nothing should be coming out of your mouth.*

5. **The deer-in-the-headlights look.** I sometimes coach political candidates and officeholders. These speakers face particularly tough questions every day, and they need to look confident while responding. The same goes for you and me. Your facial expression—especially the look in your eyes—shows others what's going on in your head. So look confident when you're asked a

tough question—rather than becoming the deer who is now staring into the headlights of your questioner's car bearing down on them—by thinking: "I can answer that!"

Now understand, it doesn't really matter if you *can* answer the question or not. Your confidence and ability to do so will show in your eyes. That puts you halfway to convincing the viewer that you really know what you're talking about. Then simply tie the question to the point you wanted to make anyway, and make it. This technique is called "bridging."

IMPORTANT ADVICE REGARDING Q & A AND INTERVIEWS: **ANSWER TOPICS, NOT QUESTIONS.** THAT WAY YOU WILL STAY IN CONTROL, RATHER THAN BEING IN A DEFENSIVE MODE CONTINUALLY CHASING AFTER QUESTIONS. YOU'LL DO A MUCH BETTER JOB OF STATING THE POINTS YOU CAME INTO THIS INTERVIEW TO MAKE, AND THAT YOU PREPARED BEFOREHAND.

6. **Revealing that you really aren't interested.** Do you pick up on cues someone may be giving you when they are totally uninterested in what you're saying? It's hard not to! By the same logic, you should avoid looking bored or condescending toward questions from your audience. Sometimes, we respond unkindly to people who just need a little more help in understanding us. Learn how to be generous and kind to anyone who has shown you respect by listening to you. Then stay engaged enough

to answer a question with sincerity, or even to follow-up with a question of your own.

7. **Leaning away.** One of the worst pieces of body language advice (usually given by self-styled "experts") is that crossed arms indicate resistance. What if the person is shifting position to be more comfortable? What if the room is cold? Leaning away from someone may not necessarily mean avoidance, either. But if it's done for long enough or is abrupt, it can indicate a definite lack of engagement or agreement.

8. **Reluctance to communicate.** Occasionally in my work as a speech coach, I work with a client who has a tight jaw. The place where your lower jaw or *mandible* meets the upper jaw or *maxilla* consists of muscles and tendons that allow smooth movement. A tight jaw, on the other hand, can indicate a reluctance to communicate, since *something* appears to be keeping you from opening up. Are you in this tribe of tight-jawed speakers? If you are, massage the area where the two jaws meet until you can open your mouth more to let your wise words out!

9. **Excessive nodding.** Here's an interesting habit that you may not be aware of. If you nod while an audience member is asking a long question—especially if you begin doing it when the question starts to *become* long, or your nodding gets more vigorous—it's a subtle 'tell' that reveals this thinking: "Yes, okay. Would you please shut up now so I can answer the question?" Be careful of showing this disrespectful behavior!

10. **Staying away from your audience.** Physical obstacles like high stages and lecterns (podiums) make it hard to connect with audiences. Worse is when we ourselves create the metaphorical or actual distance. Pay attention to the configuration of your performance space. Then think about *how to reduce the distance between you and listeners* whenever you can. That may mean declining a lectern, using the aisle(s), or employing different parts of the stage (hint: don't neglect the downstage area closest to the audience!). You do want to *reach* your listeners, don't you?

Exercise 47: Fake-It-Till-You-Make-It: How To Broadcast Confidence (Even If You're Not Feeling Any)

When you speak and otherwise interact with others concerning important and challenging topics, you want to be in The Zone. That's the almost mystical state where you're hitting on all cylinders and everything is running along like a well-lubricated engine. Doubts and thoughts about failure are somewhere over the horizon.

But what happens when you find yourself at the other end of the spectrum? That's when you're feeling a very definite *lack* of confidence, and maybe even some fear and trepidation about "going on."

That, obviously, is when you fake it! And importantly, you do much of it through your body language, since that is the easiest and most immediate way people watching and listening to you get a sense of your authority and self-confidence.

While you may think of "faking it" as a desperate measure, this strategy has some surprisingly effective benefits. Remember: audiences and other groups (who are not mind-readers) can only respond to what they see and hear. And as we already know, non-verbal communication—with its clear and strong visual clues—is almost always believed over anything that is being said. That means we believe the head nod when the person is saying, "No"; we hear doubt in a voice even though the speaker intended the sound of certainty; and a look in a speaker's eyes can alert us to untrustworthiness or lack of empathy...or the exact opposite in either case.

"Fudging" It to Create Confidence. Fortunately, faking it where body language is concerned is fairly easy. Just a few simple techniques provide the cues people need to have confidence in us.

For instance, try this simple experiment in a practice session—keeping in mind how it will look to any group of people you might be in front of later:

Stand and expel all the air from your lungs until they are completely empty.

What did that simple action do to your posture?

You probably assumed a concave or "caved in" appearance, making you appear weak and irresolute. Now, slowly fill your lungs up to their full capacity. ...Did that straighten you up? Do you feel more capable, prepared, *stronger*? I bet you do — and I guarantee that's how your audience will perceive you! (This applies to sitting down as well.)

You just used a quick technique or "trick" of combining breathing, posture, and stance to boost your level of credibility and authority with an audience. Incredible, isn't it?

Summoning a Sense of Importance and Power. It's all part of knowing how to *command space*. And you have to do it when you're in front of us so that we have confidence in you (and you have confidence in yourself). Doing so is a fast avenue to listeners' perception of you as a professional of importance and power.

And develop the habit of making CONTINUOUS EYE CONTACT with the person or people you're speaking to (including—importantly—looking straight into the webcam of your computer in a video conference). This webcam thing takes some getting used to, since in a conversation, it's the speaker who looks away more frequently than the listener. Presumably, however, everything you say is important whether you're speaking in-person or virtually. So, you need to look the others in the eye to make sure your remark or comment has the full force of your authority!

THE CONCEPT AND PRACTICE OF COMMANDING SPACE

There's more to being an authoritative speaker than just contributing to a discussion. At these moments, you must not only occupy space as you do your thing, but *control* it. As the person who holds the floor, i.e., as the leader at the moment, you're expected to show your authority physically as well as intellectually.

The Art and Practice of Physical Presence. Most of us get too wrapped up in our content—and our nervousness—when we speak in public. If we think about physical performance at all, it's to reflect how uncomfortable we are in front of all these people, and to wish we knew what to do with our hands and arms!

Yet powerful speakers go far beyond this elementary awareness of nonverbal communication. They understand how physical presence has a profound effect on their credibility and believability.

Commanding space simply means using the space that is yours when you speak. When you combine physical expressiveness—by moving to different parts of the space, gesturing, approaching listeners, and delivering your remarks at your own pace—you clearly positively influence listeners toward you and your message. Such a speaker has a tremendous advantage over a "talking head," who exhibits no dynamism whatsoever. The more comfortable you appear to be as you stand and move, the more we will identify with you, admire you, and accept what you're saying.

Not feeling the burn yet? Take a look again at the previous paragraph concerning using physical expressiveness. Is it so hard to do those things? If you do, then you'll be using an easy yet powerful way to make "faking it" work for you!

BEHAVIORAL ACTIVATION is a psychological term related to this concept. It means behaviors which are suggested to the client "with the expectation that [they] will modify or ease some painful emotion they might be experiencing."[8]

There's no need for you to wait until a make-or-break moment in an important presentation or other appearance for you to try the Fake-It-Till-You-Make-It trick, however. You can experiment with what it feels like to consciously stand and move powerfully—not emotionally moved to do so, but in a purely strategic decision. Once you have that in your grasp, then *transfer those muscle memories on stage with you later.*

Here's how you can make it happen fairly easily: Simply pay attention to what it feels like for you physically when you're doing something familiar and enjoyable and that you're committing yourself to. (It can be anything from washing your car to shoot-ing hoops to chopping wood.) At times like these, you move eas-ily and effortlessly (and often powerfully), with a clear sense of direction and forward momentum…and without hesitation. Those are the kinds of things we need to see in your physical expressiveness in front of others!

Commit those physical sensations to your muscle-memory. Now recreate them at will as you pretend you're standing in front of an audience.

Congratulations! You've just started the process of teaching your body to broadcast power, confidence, and enjoyment as a speaker, even if you don't feel those things internally. (But don't be surprised if you *start* to feel them when you begin moving and taking charge of your space!)

Exercise 48: How to Strengthen What You Say Through Gestures

Do you worry about gestures in terms of looking confident and being effective when you speak in public?

Gestures often *are* on people's minds if they are anxious about appearing in front of others. For some reason, what we do with our hands becomes magnified in our own minds in these cir-cumstances. What used to be a part of our body we didn't think much about—our arms and hands—becomes centrally impor-tant, and we begin to wonder if we're using them in the right way. It's almost as if someone just handed us those body parts and now we're wondering: "What am I supposed to do with *these*?"

In fact, one of the questions most often asked of speech coaches is: "What should I do with my hands?"

The answer is, not much.

Seriously.

Consciously considering how you should gesture is, in fact, an unnatural preoccupation that ends up calling attention to itself. Gestures need to grow out of the *feeling* that you need to say something in a stronger fashion *at this moment*—you might say, when the spirit moves you! If instead of listening closely to you, people are paying attention to the way you hold yourself and move (because you've calculated it beforehand and it looks artificial), your influence is not going to be what you'd been hoping for.

The Secret of Strong, Natural Gestures. So, what's the secret of using strong, natural gestures in public speaking? I'd say the answer is something akin to blissful ignorance. What I mean, *literally*, is that you should forget about gestures and the other ways you move your body when you speak. Listeners and audiences, after all, have no interest in them if they're tuned in to what you're telling them. It's when your physical expressiveness *amplifies or empowers* what you're saying that your gesture or movement work exactly the way they are supposed to.

Try this out now: Think of something you might say aloud later that you feel strongly about—something close to your heart that you'll really want to convince people of. At first, just say it, standing still with your arms at your sides. Now, try some things. Use a strong gesture (almost any will do) at what *feels* like the moment to do so. Don't calculate, and don't even worry about anything looking realistic at the moment...just react with your arms and hands to that feeling or concept that needs "punching up." (E.g., "Let's not EVER say that again to the management team, okay? It makes our team look RIDICULOUS!") Whatever you're saying, there is a word or phrase there that in the theater we call the "operative word"—the one that really taps into the power of what you're trying to get across.

The key to empowering the operative word (or phrase) is not to fashion a gesture to accompany it *but to create the conditions for the gesture*, i.e., the mental and emotional impetus. That will spur you to use *a* gesture at just the right time, and one that is probably of the right size and shape to punch up that important phrase or concept.

Here's another way to think of it: GESTURE ONLY WHEN YOU CAN'T *NOT* GESTURE ANY LONGER. That is, if you're completely focused on your message and getting it across to listeners, your gesture will emerge at the instant it will have the most power, because not using it simply won't express how strong the idea or concept is!

A second secret where effective gestures are concerned: The most natural position for speaking in front of an audience is with one's hands at one's sides. Your arms should simply hang neutrally. From there, you can bring your hands into play when a gesture is absolutely needed—as I said above, when you positively can't avoid it any longer. That gesture will look necessary and true to your audience.

Try this as practice: Stand up, and let your arms hang still at your sides. It may feel awkward at first, but it looks perfectly natural from the audience's perspective. Now start to speak, bringing your hands up to make a gesture only when it feels exactly right to do so. *That* gesture is a natural hand movement that fully supports whatever it is you just said.

Now, what about ineffective gestures, or speakers who gesture too much? Here's a General Rule to remember along these lines:

ANY MOVEMENT THAT REINFORCES OR AMPLIFIES YOUR MESSAGE IS GOOD, AND ANY MOVEMENT THAT DETRACTS FROM YOUR MESSAGE IS NOT. Keep this rule in mind, and you won't find yourself pulling on your ear every third sentence, or making uplifting hand gestures that seem to be saying, "I need to throw up, but nothing's coming!"

FINDING YOUR CENTER

One last comment to help you gesture with precision and power. (And of course, gestures that are few in number and well defined will always be more effective than using too many hand movements.)

Learn how to make your gestures come from your center, not from "the fringes." A mirror will help you here. Imagine an invisible box—similar to, say, the strike zone in baseball, but a bit smaller. This "box" goes from shoulder to shoulder, and downward to your waist. *All of your gestures should emerge from inside this box, and no gestures should start outside of the box.*

In this way, your gestures emerge from "the center of you"... which is exactly where ALL of your physical and emotional presence should come from. Keep the gestures tight and strong, and don't allow them to go too far outside the box (though slightly outside is okay). Especially avoid letting your arms and hands flail in the air, far away from your core. And try never to use gestures that are above your shoulders. You'll just be tossing away energy from your center, where good speakers keep things emerging and showing how visual concepts illustrate ideas.

Exercise 49: Getting Comfortable With Your Body

I mentioned in Chapter 4 that, rather than body language, I like to use the term "physical expression." To me, it's a reminder that our bodies are communication tools that are essential parts of how we express ourselves. The fact that speaking in public tends to inhibit our physical expressiveness is just something we need to recognize and get over.

You're comfortable with your body when you're not self-conscious about it, aren't you? Actually, that's a key point to keep in mind if you tend to be overly aware and a bit dissatisfied with how you look and move in front of others. Think about how your physical presence, movements, and gestures work when you're with friends or colleagues, or in any situation where you're relaxed and *not thinking* about your physicality.

Let's face it: these are the times when you look and move exactly like who you are. There's no conscious plan or strategy going on ("I have to look unconcerned about that problem"). You simply respond physically to what you're feeling and thinking. Incidentally, this is also a good method of understanding how physical expression works—that you *naturally* and *energetically* respond physically based on what you're saying (or in some cases, thinking). Your body language in these situations is definitely *not* based on what you think you will look like, so that you end up planning it ahead of time!

If you want to be effective in terms of using physical expression in formal, i.e., business and other situations, simply bring *that* physically unconscious person on stage with you—the unpremeditated one. You should never plan your gestures or reactions ahead of time. (You can and should, however, scope out where you want to stand on stage so that each of your main points has maximum impact). Choreographing your gestures beforehand simply makes them look calculated and fake. Instead, CREATE THE FEELING OR CONDITIONS FOR THE GESTURE, and the one that emerges will be honest and true.

For instance, when you get to the point where you reveal your brand's new advertising software to your corporate customers, the moment of your "big reveal" should look fresh, spontaneous, and exciting. Trust yourself to use a strong, natural gesture that taps into that, and it will be the right one!

To put it as simply as possible: get out of your head and into your body.

Exercise 50: Using Your Body to Communicate

The term is "body language." So what *is* the language of the body?

Well, it's exactly like your speaking, i.e., expressing yourself moment by moment. In this case, you're doing it physically *as well as* orally.

Again, it isn't something you necessarily think about. It's more a case of tuning into all of the stimuli coming your way. That includes your own sense of your body in space; your breathing; and the sound of your voice. You should even be responding to the physical environment you share with the audience. Watch your listeners' reactions.

If you're speaking virtually and there isn't a shared space or you can't see the listeners, pay particular attention to how the ideas of your presentation are changing, and use those changes as new stimuli (as in fact they are!). That means allowing your physical voice to reflect your thoughts and ideas in a way that is slightly different from how you were using it on your last point. There's a continuous dance going on between you and your audience. Don't stand against the wall (as it were) where no one can appreciate you. Step out, participate, and enjoy it!

Too often, we're so absorbed in our desire to do well that we don't pay attention to each moment that we and the audience share that will *allow* us to be effective. Most of the time, we give all our attention to our material, and *none* to how our listeners will respond to it. For instance, many times because of how nervous we are, we over-prepare. We put together a carefully constructed presentation *so that nothing can go wrong.* Then we roll it out *in spite* of the audience. You can easily see that in a situation like this, we're not responding to the speaking moment at all!

Listen to Your Limbic System! If you open yourself up to it instead—if you let the moment happen—you'll connect with your limbic system (see Chapter 3), which is all about processing the moment and shaping your emotional response to it. Don't worry about losing control over your material. If you know your stuff, you'll be able to deliver the content to listeners more naturally than a rigid presentation ever could.

Your limbic brain is an incredible tool that helps give you presence, provided that you listen to what it's telling you. The result can be physical expressiveness that is perfectly calibrated for the moment at hand.

EXTERNALIZING WHAT YOU FEEL

And here's a key point. It's one of the most valuable lessons you as a businessperson can learn from the actor: the need to physically express what you're thinking and feeling. Here's the key to this idea:

YOU MUST SHOW OUTWARDLY WHAT'S GOING ON INSIDE YOU, OR YOUR AUDIENCE WILL NEVER BE ABLE TO THINK AND FEEL THE SAME THINGS THEMSELVES.

They aren't mind-readers!

This ability to externalize what's inside you is perhaps the central skill of acting, and it's a quality that is often lacking in public speakers. It's not hard to understand why. Actors train and rehearse their entire professional lives to be able to physically externalize mental and emotional states. It's a skill of spoken performance that, sadly, almost no one in business is ever exposed to.

Accept this truth then: if you want to achieve leadership presence, you must speak in the language of the body as well as that of the mind. Body language is the art of physical expression, and it's as vital to your influence as anything you say.

How to Be at Ease Using Body Language. Want an easy way to adopt this powerful performance tool while increasing your comfort level in front of an audience? Imagine you're welcoming listeners into your living room. You know what it's like to be at ease in your own environment, welcoming friends through the front door. Use this visualization to bring your audience into the space (real or virtual) that you'll be occupying together.

If you can project that level of comfort, audiences will feel they're in good hands. And why not? What they'll see and hear is your true voice and natural physical expression on a topic everyone is interested in. In the best way possible, you'll be 'embodying' the content you're sharing with them.

BUILDING TRUST AND EMPATHY: FACIAL EXPRESSIONS

To conclude this chapter on body language and physical display, I'd like to talk about facial expressions. This is often a neglected topic when it comes to understanding the body in performance.

If you're like most people, you focus mainly on your gestures when it comes to using body language for public speaking. But what your face is showing gives your audience important clues about everything from your passion for the topic to whether you're a trustworthy messenger. And believe me, audiences are keenly aware of what they're seeing and how it relates to their own needs. Animals rely on a keen sense of smell for recognition and to sense danger. But we *watch* each other's faces and bodies to try to understand feelings and intentions.

And the face is easily as expressive as the body! We're capable of thousands of facial expressions, including fifty different types of smiles.[9] Therefore, as a speaker, you need a sense of what your own face is showing in performance.

Is your face flexible enough to show what you're feeling? Or do you lack much facial expression? Public speaking isn't a poker game where the object is to hide what you're thinking! And when you do show emotion, are your expressions appropriate?

A key question for any speaker is whether audiences are seeing what he or she is really thinking. No speaker wants listeners to have a false impression based on what his or her face is showing. Many of my clients, in fact, are shocked when they see themselves on video. They are often observing for the first time not only what they look like overall, but what they're sending out as facial signals. If it's the opposite of what they intended, it can be quite unsettling.

To see this in action, try videotaping or screen-recording yourself on a topic you typically speak on. Make sure the topic is important to you—the more heartfelt advocacy it involves, the better. Deliver your remarks as though you were actually speaking in a real-life situation. Just before you watch yourself, turn off the volume or mute the microphone on your screen. Now you'll be paying more attention to your face than your content. (Also, for this exercise, try to focus on your face rather than your gestures.)

Imagine you're an audience member watching this speaker, i.e., you. Ask yourself the following questions. (1) What are you seeing in terms of this person's commitment to their message? (2) How strongly do you think she or he wants to get it across? (3) Do they seem to genuinely care about this topic? (4) Am I seeing anything that reveals how this speaker feels about his or her listeners?

You can also enlist the help of friends and colleagues by asking them what you seem to be showing facially. It can be startling at times to hear that you're showing an emotion you're not feeling at all. ("Why did you seem angry?")

But show us *something*. You're the most expressive animal on the planet![10] For us to benefit fully from what you have to give us, we need to see it facially as well as bodily.

STILLNESS AND POWER

One last thought in this chapter on physical expressiveness. Powerful stage presence starts with *stillness*. Stillness conveys confidence and control. The speaker who begins with stillness moves precisely when she or he feels the need to do so.

Just as people who babble incessantly come across as insecure next to the person who is still and composed, the nervous performer merely calls attention to the uncontrolled nature of superfluous movement.

The art of full expression comes from being in touch with what you say, how you feel about it, and how you express it, verbally and physically. After that, it's just a case of being open enough to pour it all out to us so we get it. Keep this in mind and your physical performance will be dynamic and effective—and absolutely stand out from the run-of-the-mill.

You can be confident of that.

NOTES

1   When I was a teenager, one of the nearby towns had a bowling alley. It was situated right next to a drive-in theater. The bowling alley had huge picture widows, and if you stood at one of them, you could watch the entire movie playing at the drive-in for free. Of course, you couldn't hear what anybody was saying. But, if the actors were good, you could get a pretty good idea of what was happening in the scene from their body language and other nonverbal communication.

2   Joe Navarro, What Every Body Is Saying (New York: William Morrow, 2008), 4, quoting J.K. Burgoon, D.B. Buller, and W.G. Woodall, Nonverbal Communication: The Unspoken Dialogue (Columbus, OH: Greyden Press, 1994), 229-285.

3   Albert Mehrabian, Silent Messages (Belmont, CA: Wadsworth, 1981), 75-80.

4   Daniel Goleman, Emotional Intelligence (New York: Bantam, 1995), 97.

5   https://en.wikipedia.org/wiki/Jill_Bolte_Taylor.

6   Amy Cuddy, Presence (New York: Little, Brown Spark, 2018), 40.

7   Carmine Gallo. Talk Like TED (New York: St. Martin's Griffin, 2014), 90. Quoting Morgan Wright, Chief Crime Fighter, Washington, D.C. Metro Area, in discussion with the author, April 4, 2013.

8   Caroline Bologna, "'Fake It Till You Make It' Isn't Just a Cliché. It's Backed By Science," Huffpost, August 3, 2022. https://www. huffpost.com/entry/behavioral-activation-fake-it-til-you-make-it_l_62d7140ae4b0aad58d139763

9   Paul Ekman, Telling Lies (New York: W.W. Norton, 1992), 127.

10 Navarro, 165.

CHAPTER 11

How Your Voice Transforms Your Relationships

The 2010 film "The King's Speech" about stammering King George VI of England taught audiences about the power of one's personal voice. Each of us—whether we're a sales rep, football coach giving a pep talk at halftime, or President of the United States—needs to have faith in our own voice. The truth is, it's not only what we say but the unique way we say it that gives legitimacy to our speech—pretty spectacular evidence that we all possess an inborn talent to speak with originality and effectiveness.

Faith in your voice, then, should give you tremendous confidence as a speaker. Your voice is exceptional because it is yours alone. No one—not the King of England himself!—can speak in your voice and give listeners what they need to hear.

Exercise 51: The Wonder of Your Voice: Using It to Influence Listeners

This chapter of *The Confidence Book* will show you how to give free and full expression to your vocal uniqueness to positively influence listeners. Doing so is a powerful tool for increasing your self-confidence. When you believe in your own voice, you cannot be silenced—not even by your own fears and perceived inadequacies in other areas.

You must also bear in mind, however, that you will never be a perfect speaker, so you shouldn't place that burden on yourself. Such a creature doesn't exist! You'll actually be something much more interesting: a speaker who goes beyond the mere delivery of information to express who you are fundamentally. In the end, that's what audiences are looking for. When you can *get out of your own way* as a speaker, everything you have to offer will come through clearly and powerfully. This chapter will help you find ways to make that happen vocally.

ARE YOU SINGING YOUR SPEECH OR JUST MOUTHING THE WORDS?

Did you ever consider that delivering an outstanding presentation is like performing a great song? Not only is the "music" delightful to listen to, but your voice soars on a combination of dynamic technique and an inspirational message. The way you use your vocal tools carries astonishing weight with regard to credibility, authority, and that all-important attribute, believability.

Why does your voice alone make such a difference? Well, for one thing, we all respond in basic and even primitive ways to the qualities of a person's voice. If a voice is pleasant and authoritative, for instance, it inspires confidence in the listener. But a voice that comes across as unpleasant, weak, or too timid nudges that same listener in the opposite direction.

Vocal dynamics, or vocal variety, is one of the most effective tools you own for winning over audiences in that positive direction. The elements of vocal dynamics—tone quality, pitch placement, inflection, use of emphasis, variations in pace and tempo, pauses, and all the emotional nuances your voice can project—provide a nearly limitless palette to "paint word pictures" and convince others. When you employ good vocal dynamics, you make your stories and ideas come vibrantly alive for your listeners.

The Potential of Your Voice. One effective way to realize your vocal potential is to keep in mind that the voice is inherently physical. That fact may sound obvious, but it's easy to forget when you as speaker are preoccupied with the content of your presentation or consumed by performance anxiety. (You may also confuse "verbal" with "vocal," as many people do, since both words begin with "v" and refer to what comes out of your mouth when you speak. This is how to remember the difference: VERBAL refers to *what* you say, while VOCAL deals with *how you say it*.)

Because your voice is physical, it is directly connected to energy and relaxation, as well as tension and stress. That means that the pressures of a too-hectic lifestyle or work schedule will probably emerge in one form or another as diminished vocal quality. Anything you can do to relieve those pressures—yoga, sports, relaxation exercises, adequate hydration—will pay off in a more flexible and powerful vocal instrument.

Getting to 'Flow'. Of course, in addition to being relaxed vocally, you must have something worthwhile to say. Neither beautiful words without meaning, nor the passionate delivery of a package empty of ideas will lead to success.

The power of your message, then, hinges on your ability to combine three things: (1) your message, (2) vocal quality, and (3) nonverbal communication. Like every good speaker, you must tie your material to your vocal delivery and body language, linking together all three speech elements. Here's an easy way to remember this idea. It applies to delivering presentations, pitches, updates, advocacy, and any other remarks: *You should fully commit to your message, express it passionately, and use supportive body language and gestures.* Who wouldn't be persuaded or at least attentive to such a speaker?

Just as important: which of those speakers wouldn't have confidence in their own abilities if they encompassed those three things every time they speak? I'm talking to *you* here!

The Voice is Your Perfect Tool for Power, Expressiveness, and Confidence. Once you're aware of your personal potential for vocal power and expressiveness, you can learn how to more subtly influence your audience. For the *suppleness* and *flexibility* of the vocal instrument is a vital factor in persuasion that is most often ignored! If you can speak with this ability, you will absolutely separate yourself from the herd.

Because it embodies so many attributes concerning range, subtlety, adaptability, personalization, even intimacy ("Let me whisper the secret of this sales deal to you,") your voice can build trust; instill confidence in a product, service, or idea; create excitement among listeners; motivate them to act; increase their positive feelings toward you; and achieve many other positive outcomes that our other in-person communication tools cannot.

Of course, for these changes to occur, your audience must trust and respect you as a speaker. That means you need to have an honest conversation with your listeners, not spin them or "speechify" to them using fancy rhetoric, or especially, use your vocal powers to manipulate them.

What's the Best Way to Sound Natural? What's the best way to sound natural and trustworthy so you can have such an honest conversation with others? It's to allow them to hear who you truly are, not try to impress them. And it starts with using the VOCAL PITCH that's right for you.

Many people don't. Find out below how *you* can!

Exercise 52: Finding Your Optimal Pitch

"Pitch" in terms of speech refers to the voice's highness or lowness on the musical scale. The size of one's vocal cords plays a role here. But so does the amount of tension present: the more tension in evidence, the higher the pitch will be because the vocal cords will be tight. Think of a guitar string: the more the string is "stopped" (shortened), the higher the musical note sounded will be.

Finding the pitch that's right for you is important, because the less tension you bring to your throat, the more relaxed your actual voice will be. For the sake of the exercise which follows, you also need one more piece of information. You need to understand the terms HABITUAL PITCH and OPTIMAL PITCH.

It May Be a Habit. But Is It Optimal? We all speak at a certain pitch (highness or lowness) out of habit. That is our *habitual pitch*. But sometimes, that pitch is putting a strain on our voice and preventing vocalization from being effortless, or carrying far enough to reach all of the audience members. In other words, we're not using our *optimal pitch.*

Have you ever wondered if the pitch you use when you speak was the right one for you? We're going to explore the answer to that question below.

The Way Men and Women Speak. Males and females sometimes use a habitual pitch that isn't optimal for them, for opposite reasons. Men can have a tendency to *sit* on their pitch, forcing it down into lower registers to sound more masculine. Women, on the other hand, sometimes head in the opposite direction. They may use a light and girlish voice that they learned to use to be "well behaved" when they were young, but now may not match their level of maturity.

So it's worth knowing whether the pitch you're in the habit of using is right for you in terms of vocal health and the best sound production. Here are two quick-and-easy methods of discovering your optimal pitch, regardless of the pitch you're using now out of habit:

DISCOVERING YOUR OPTIMAL PITCH

METHOD A: Without thinking about it beforehand, record yourself singing "Happy Birthday" (you can finish it with "...to Me" or anyone else's name!) Once you've sung "Happy Birthday," and without stopping the tape, immediately record yourself talking about the things you have to accomplish at work this week or next week, using your normal voice. Now play back the recording. The song and the spoken passage should be at *about the same pitch,* with neither one significantly higher or lower than the other. If they aren't, your rendition of "Happy Birthday" is closer to your optimal pitch, since it was presumably spontaneous and you didn't think about it. (Most of us have a tendency to become more serious-sounding when we're discussing business and therefore unconsciously lower our pitch.)

Method B: Sing a sustained note somewhere in the middle of your vocal range. Now "step down" one note on the musical scale at a time starting at the top, i.e., "Do," "Ti," "La," "Sol," and so on. Continue until you reach *the lowest note you can sustain without your voice breaking up.* Now come up two or three notes on the scale. That should be close to your optimal pitch.

If you just discovered that your habitual pitch (the one you're in the habit of using) doesn't match your optimal pitch (your healthiest and most effective pitch), make any necessary adjustments to get closer to your optimal pitch. Then remember to use your optimal pitch as often as possible.

Do this in practice sessions where you can record yourself and listen back. In actual presentations or meetings, don't even think about it, because you have other things on your mind you need to be attending to. The idea is to eventually make speaking at *your optimal pitch* your new *habitual pitch*! Just knowing you're doing this should give you the confidence that you're using the pitch that's best for you.

Exercise 53: Boost Your Vocal Impact with These 5 Key Vocal Tools

THE 5 ESSENTIAL TOOLS OF VOCAL EXPRESSIVENESS

Now that you've found the pitch that's right for you, it's time to learn about the ingredients that will add variety and flavor to your voice. No one likes bland food, and the same principle applies to the vocal banquet you're serving up for your listeners.

There are many advantages to having a lively and expressive voice. They include audiences perceiving that you have more impact and power, warmth, audibility, authority, trustworthiness, passion, intelligence, and assertiveness, among other attributes. Together these qualities will dramatically improve your ability to engage and influence listeners.

To practice them, you need to know how to use five essential vocal tools:

1. **Emphasis and energy**
2. **Pitch inflection**
3. **Variety in rhythm and pacing**
4. **Pauses and silence**
5. **Vocal quality**

Let's look at each of these in turn.

1. **Emphasis and energy** is concerned with the *force or stress* you place on important ideas, concepts, or feelings, as well as a generally energized vocal style. It is the simplest of the 5 essential vocal tools, and one that you probably already know how to use well.

2. **Pitch inflection** refers to the rising and falling of your pitch on the musical scale. Sometimes called *intonation*, lively pitch inflection helps you avoid monotony as well as convey meaning. It's not only a critically important vocal tool; it's the one you may have the most trouble using freely in formal speaking situations. (Generally speaking, it's the weakest area of the five vocal tools for individuals like

business people and other professionals.) If you haven't received performance training in the use of the voice, that is, you may have a tendency to stay in a too-narrow pitch range, limiting your voice's natural ability to express emotion. (This is related to my earlier comment that when it comes time to speak professionally, too many people become "all business," and their voice flattens out in an attempt to sound serious. I've heard this effect thousands of time in business and other professional speakers…and so have you.)

There's another possibility if you find that your voice has a 'flat' quality when you speak in public. It might be self-consciousness that's inhibiting your ability to vary your pitch enough to convey emotional content. If this is the case, I'd be willing to bet that you don't use such an expressionless voice when you're telling a joke to friends or explaining to your spouse what's making you angry! It's that "Now I have to sound businesslike, without any passion" trap again!

3. Your **rhythm and pace** also need to be varied when you speak publicly so your audience stays attentive and aware of the nuances of what you're saying. In normal conversation, i.e., when you're not self-conscious, your speaking rhythm changes frequently according to new ideas or emotions you bring up. Why should it be any different when you're giving a presentation? If you've ever suffered through a talk by a presenter who speaks in metronomic fashion, you know how an unvaried pace can lull an audience into inattention.

4. **Pauses and silence** is another vocal tool you may be neglecting, this time due to speech anxiety. Pauses in a speech can add emphasis, build suspense, bridge ideas, make a comment on what you just said, and enrich your talk in other subtle ways. If you pause at appropriate times, you'll also show your audience that you're confident enough to set the pace for yourself rather than rushing through your talk because of nervousness. Unfortunately, adrenaline by its nature forces you to either fight the "threat" you're facing or run from it—in other words, taking any course of action rather than *pausing!*

Pauses are essential in two instances: (1) when you've just said something important that needs time to sink in, and (2) when you transition between main talking points. Different ideas and information segments can flow together unnoticeably if you're not careful, confusing listeners. (That is, *you* know how your speech is shaped and how each main point builds on and leads into the next, but your listeners don't have a clue unless you give them some help. One of the best ways to do so is to simply pause between each change of idea, alerting them that something new is coming.) By pausing before you start on your next point, you'll allow your audience to prime themselves to receive new information—to take a mental breath and "hit the reset button," rather than miss the point because they think it's part of the same previous topic. It's part of USING YOUR PERFORMANCE SKILLS TO BUILD ON THE VERBAL CONTENT, WHICH IS NEVER ENOUGH ON ITS OWN.

5. **Vocal quality** is the last and most all-encompassing of the 5 vocal tools. It includes the tone, richness, and pleasantness of your voice, along with other factors such as breathiness, warmth or stridency, patience or impatience, empathy or anger, hesitancy or bewilderment, and other elements that affect people's emotional response to you. No wonder vocal quality is the most all-inclusive of the essential tools!

   Since it's the culminating effect which incorporates the other four tools, vocal quality is the most sophisticated vocal attribute in your toolbox. You might change your vocal quality, for instance, when you want to lead your audience to a certain emotional response—a whispered phrase to evoke mystery and suppressed emotion; or a doltish voice when you're characterizing a thick-headed person, etc. Those are the kinds of effects that a changed vocal quality can elicit.

   Use These Tools As a Package. The key to the 5 essential vocal tools is that they should be used *together* rather than in isolation, for that's when they work best. Now that you know what they are, use them all because they are fully and easily at your disposal at all times. If you do, your audiences will stay tuned more easily, pay closer attention to what you're saying, and find themselves more easily moved and persuaded.

Exercise 54: Bringing Ideas and Emotions to Life

PASSAGES TO PRACTICE FOR VOCAL EXPRESSIVENESS

Now it's time for you to practice! The following exercises, which include prose, poetry, and song passages, are rich in opportunities for you to use all of the vocal tools you just learned about in the previous exercise on the key techniques of vocal expressiveness. You should, of course, read these passages aloud. In fact, they *demand* that you do. That's why this kind of writing is an excellent vehicle for shaking out your vocal apparatus and getting it *going*. Once you hear your voice coming to life with much greater variety and color (as demanded by these selections), you can apply your new proficiency to your professional remarks and presentations. Granted, your business content will probably be much less dramatic. But the vocal effects that you use are exactly the same—you simply decide when to use them based on your knowledge of what you're really trying to get across.

From *Dracula*, by Bram Stoker

I looked out over the beautiful expanse, bathed in soft yellow moonlight till it was almost as light as day. In the soft light the distant hills became melted, and the shadows in the valleys and gorges of velvety blackness. The mere beauty seemed to cheer me; there was peace and comfort in every breath I drew. As I leaned from the window my eye was caught by something moving a storey below me, and somewhat to my left, where I imagined, from the order of the rooms that the windows of the Count's own room would look out. The window at which I stood was tall and deep, stone-mullioned [pronounced "MULL-yunned"], and though weather worn, was still complete; but it was evidently many a day since the case had been there. I drew back behind the stonework, and looked carefully out.

What I saw was the Count's head coming out from the window. I did not see the face, but I knew the man by the neck and the movement of his back and arms. In any case I could not mistake the hands which I had had so many opportunities of studying. I was at first interested and somewhat amused, for it is wonderful how small a matter will interest and amuse a man when he is a prisoner. But my very feelings changed to repulsion and terror when I saw the whole man slowly emerge from the window and begin to crawl down the castle wall over that dreadful abyss, *face down*, with his cloak spreading out around him like great wings. At first I could not believe my eyes. I thought it was some trick of the moonlight, some weird effect of shadow; but I kept looking, and it could be no delusion. I saw the fingers and toes grasp the corners of the stones, worn clear of the mortar by the stress of years, and by thus using every projection and inequality move downwards with considerable speed, just as a lizard moves along a wall.

What manner of man is this, or what manner of creature is it in the semblance of man? I feel the dread of this horrible place overpowering me; I am in fear—in awful fear—and there is no escape for me....

COMMENTARY: Did you notice the *transitions* in this passage—the places where the mood, idea, or images change, sometimes radically? Transitions *always* point to places where your vocal "flavor" needs to be different. That's because **the need for your voice to reflect the changing ideas or emotions of your content is as basic to professional communication as it is to novels and dramatic literature.** In the above passage, for instance, there are four major transitions resulting in five distinct sections concerning content (in this case, what is going on in the story as told in the diary entry being read). Go back to the piece and see if you can identify them!

Now Use *All* of the Vocal Tools. Speak the selection again, this time allowing your voice to fully reflect what you (i.e., the narrator) are thinking and feeling at each stage as you describe these incredible events. This is not acting, since you're not being asked to *become* this person (his name is Jonathan Harker) in a stage performance. But you *will be* closer to employing the actor's toolbox of a fully expressive and active voice!

Use the same approach with the selections that follow.

From *Romeo and Juliet,* by William Shakespeare

Our second selection is from *Romeo and Juliet.* Romeo Montague, having overcome his schoolboy crush on another girl, realizes that Juliet Capulet, the daughter of his family's sworn enemies, is the young lady he is destined to love. Hiding in the Capulets' orchard at night, he sees Juliet appear at a window. His soliloquy, incidentally, is an ideal piece to practice "supporting your words," i.e., having enough breath to finish a phrase. (Look over Exercise 7, "Are You Breathing Incorrectly?" again in Chapter 2 on Breathing Techniques to remind yourself that you must use enough breath to "punch" whatever comes at the *ends* of the ideas you're expressing. Remember, in English, the most important words or phrases usually come at the end of the idea or concept, not the beginning or middle.)

In this piece and in whatever you say professionally, bear that in mind—give these words or phrases the clarity and emphasis they demand through your voice. That means having enough breath left to do so! Otherwise, enjoy speaking through the rhythms and emphases Shakespeare has given you.[1]

But, soft! what light through yonder window breaks?
It is the east, and Juliet is the sun.
Arise, fair sun, and kill the envious moon,
Who is already sick and pale with grief,
That thou her maid art far more fair than she:
Be not her maid, since she is envious;
Her vestal livery is but sick and green
And none but fools do wear it; cast it off.
It is my lady, O, it is my love!
O, that she knew she were!
She speaks yet she says nothing: what of that?
Her eye discourses; I will answer it.
I am too bold, 'tis not to me she speaks:
Two of the fairest stars in all the heaven,
Having some business, do entreat her eyes

To twinkle in their spheres till they return.
What if her eyes were there, they in her head?
The brightness of her cheek would shame those stars,
As daylight doth a lamp; her eyes in heaven
Would through the airy region stream so bright
That birds would sing and think it were not night.
See, how she leans her cheek upon her hand!
O, that I were a glove upon that hand,
That I might touch that cheek!

From *The Taming of the Shrew,* by William Shakespeare

The last vocal exercise is one you can do with a partner. In a famous scene from Shakespeare's *The Taming of the Shrew,* Petruchio, a gentleman of Verona visiting Padua, Italy, decides to woo Katharine, the "shrew" or unpleasant female of the title. Though famous for her temper, Katharine or "Kate" possesses a large dowry. Petruchio is delighted by both the challenge and the lady's riches, and vows that he will win Kate for his wife. What follows is their first encounter (if you're practicing this alone, you can speak both parts). During this verbal joust, the air is electric with sexual tension. Their repartee is therefore filled with double entendres and racy references. Have fun!

> Petruchio: Come, come, you wasp; i' faith, you are too angry.
> Katharine: If I be waspish, best beware my sting.
> Petruchio: My remedy is then, to pluck it out.
> Katharine: Ay, if the fool could find it where it lies.

Petruchio: Who knows not where a wasp
does wear his sting? In his tail.
Katharine: In his tongue.
Petruchio: Whose tongue?
Katharine: Yours, if you talk of tails; and so farewell.
Petruchio: What, with my tongue in your tail?
nay, come again,
Good Kate; I am a gentleman.
Katharine: That I'll try [i.e., test].

She strikes him.

You don't have to actually hit yourself, by the way!

Once again, notice the operative or most important words coming at the ends of the lines in this selection: angry, sting, pluck it out, lies, tail, tongue, tongue, farewell, gentleman, try (followed by the slap). Believe me, audiences had no difficulty, four hundred years ago, understanding the flirting and sexual challenges flying back and forth in this scene! In your own remarks, your listeners will similarly pick up on the important phrases that cap your ideas, especially if you're breathing diaphragmatically and have sufficient air left to express them strongly!

These practice passages for vocal expressiveness above should have made you aware of something else as well: that emotions, ideas, and the power of expression depend partly upon word position as well as how the words are expressed. For instance, in your own realm, there's a world of difference between, "Well, this opportunity is one that I think our company shouldn't pass up"; and, "Our company definitely *shouldn't pass up this opportunity!*" If you were speaking, which one would make you feel more confident that the listeners got your meaning and that you expressed it powerfully? (I even had to add an exclamation point to the second example, since it seemed to call for it.)

Part of the Work Has Been Done for You Already. Bear in mind: it isn't necessary for you to intentionally *place* important words at the end of your idea. The language you speak, English, has already placed them there for you based on what you're trying to say.

Now, apply what you've just practiced to the things you say in your speeches and presentations. Remember that, more often than not, the thing you say as you *conclude* a phrase or idea has the greatest impact, and you should make sure your listeners hear it clearly. Don't make the common error of letting your voice sink as you complete a phrase because you're getting ready to express the *next* idea in your notes or slide. The idea you're on right now still needs to come across with clarity and power to your audience.

Let's go now from the world of 16th-century drama and 19th-century horror to our own era. Below are some examples from the modern world of business, politics, and sports so you can see why supporting an idea vocally is essential. The italics are mine, added to point out what we've been talking about for a while now: that the important ideas in these quotes occur at the ends of phrases:

- "Tonight, all of our men and women in uniform—in Iraq, Afghanistan and around the world—must know that they have our respect, our gratitude, *and our full support.*"[2]

- "Now, in many respects, information has never been *so free.* There are more ways to spread more ideas to more people *than at any moment in history.*"[3]

- "Are we ready for tomorrow, *today*? For the next day and a half, you're going to see, first-hand, how *we are shaping the future—today.*"[4]

- "One of my goals has always been *never to work a day in my life.* I don't consider what I do as work, because every day that I train and compete, I find *even greater joy in the process.*"[5]

Exercise 55: Using a Warmer and More Pleasant Voice

Ever find yourself unpleasantly surprised by someone you admired but had never heard speak?

That happened to me recently. I was researching an upcoming conference, and since I'm a speech coach, was interested in one of the keynote speakers. But I was somewhat shocked when I found this person online and listened to one of his speeches.

Your Voice Is a Key Factor in Business Success. This keynote speaker was obviously successful (he'd been allotted one of the high-profile speaking slots), even though he had a poor vocal style. Of course, we all want to be successful in our careers. But who wants to be known as a high-achiever who, unfortunately, can't speak in public very well?

People respond to your voice in ways that predate modern speech by hundreds of thousands of years. Critical factors in influencing people—including likability, trustworthiness, credibility, expertise, and the ability to work well on a team, among others—depend in part on how you sound when you speak.

So if you haven't done any self-improvement work in this

area, perhaps it's time to get started. Below are 5 ways you can strengthen one essential component of an engaging speaking style: a warm and pleasant voice. Let's look at how you can consciously work toward improving this winning aspect of your voice so that people will respond to you positively.

1. BREATHE DIAPHRAGMATICALLY FOR A MORE PLEASANT SOUND

You already know from Exercise 6 in Chapter 2 about diaphragmatic breathing. You've learned that it's a key skill in achieving a powerful voice while reducing speech anxiety, nervousness, and fear. It's also an asset in knowing how to boost your focus and presence, since "coming back" to your breathing automatically re-positions you in the present moment and time, where you can be most effective.

For the purposes of this chapter, you should know that natural breathing also helps create a softer and more pleasant sound in your voice. That's because, by getting a full reservoir of air into your lungs—through breathing diaphragmatically—you provide yourself with a "cushion" of air that helps lessen the sound of a harsh or nasal voice. (That, incidentally, was my main complaint with the speaker I found online).

Here's another benefit to what a fully oxygenated voice can do for you. You can try this now to immediately hear the difference yourself. First, eliminate nearly all the air in your lungs. Now try to say something as if you were speaking to a crowd in a large room like a hotel ballroom. Not much power in that voice, is there? Now, let your diaphragm descend (remember, your tummy comes out) so your lungs can fill up completely. Now say the same thing to that same imaginary crowd. Your voice carries easily, doesn't it, reaching everyone with a full, pleasurable sound with no strain in it at all?

2. BALANCE YOUR HEAD AND CHEST VOICE

Have you noticed the epidemic of "little voices," in which seasoned male and female professionals in business, and especially broadcasting, sound like boys and girls instead of men and women? These are teenage voices more than anything else, without gravitas or maturity. Ira Glass, the host of the radio show "This American Life," is a good model of this. Speaking in this way is an example of *HEAD VOICE*, or speaking too thinly with the voice located only above the neck.

CHEST VOICE, on the other hand, situates the sound in the thoracic or chest cavity. This vocal style has its own benefits and drawbacks. If used exclusively, the chest voice can sound like it's stuck in an elevator a few floors down. Admittedly, this voice has heaps more wisdom and maturity to it than a head voice. But it can also have a "fuddy-duddy" or pompous quality.

The solution is a balance between the two. Combine your HEAD and CHEST voices so you achieve a balance of bright, clear sound (head voice) and a more mature and authoritative quality (chest voice). The over-brightness of too much head voice, and the dullness of too much chest voice, are avoided as you create a balance that's both warm and intelligent.

Tape yourself, and judge what you hear. First, become a "talking head" by placing your vocal sound completely between your ears (you'll hear it immediately!); then say the same thing, letting the sound sink down completely into your chest (you'll hear that too, you old grump). Finally, create the balance: literally (physically) placing your voice in between those two locations. You should hear a clear, beneficial difference in your recording.

3. RELAX YOUR VOCAL CORDS TO SOUND MORE EMPATHETIC

Once you're breathing well and you know how to create a more balanced sound, pay attention to how relaxed your vocal cords are. The vocal cords (the thyroarytenoid muscles) are actually *folds* of muscle in the larynx; and in fact they're often called *vocal folds* in medical parlance. At any rate, when you speak, exhaled air activates these cords or folds so they vibrate,[6] producing sound waves that we hear as your voice.

Like any muscles in the body, the focal folds can become tight from tension and stress. We're all good at recognizing when our shoulders are tight. But what about when the same thing is happening inside your throat?

You can easily test this yourself: Tighten your vocal cords when you speak and listen to the sound that emerges. Harsh, isn't it? Now relax them completely, using a soft, breathy, "loose" way of speaking. Your voice took on a warm, buttery sound, didn't it? You can overdo it, of course. But try making a relaxed voice more of a habit. You'll sound more empathetic and warmer toward your listeners.

4. ADJUST YOUR PACE TO MAKE THINGS EASY FOR YOUR AUDIENCE

If you're rushed as a speaker, you're putting pressure on your audience. They won't like it, and they won't feel comfortable.

You're also doing yourself a disservice. When you rush through your talk, your voice can't do its job. That includes *coloring* what you're saying, through emphasizing and de-emphasizing, pausing to create anticipation, slowing your speech to indicate the importance of key items, and a hundred other vocal effects and qualities that bring your intelligence and sensibility fully into the game. Otherwise, you're speaking in black and white rather than glorious color! Most important, you're not allowing listeners to understand your intentions and who you really are through the full coloration you bring to your vocal delivery.

5. THINK IN TERMS OF CONNECTING WITH LISTENERS

Recently, I worked with a client who is an anxious speaker. To compensate, this business owner composes her entire talks and delivers them from a meticulously written manuscript.

What's wrong with this? Nothing, if you want your audience to feel like you're reading from a script instead of just talking to them in the here-and-now.

Your job as a good communicator is always to establish a connection with your audience. *When you look at people and relate to them, your voice suddenly becomes part of the interaction.* There's all the difference in the world between someone reading off a sheet of paper or a slide versus participating in a conversation. When you make the effort to talk to an audience *exactly as if this were a conversation* (because it is!), everyone hears the result. Your warmth, your personality, and all the rest of who you are emerge. You *and* the audience will immediately hear when you're on the right wavelength.

Exercise 56: The 3-Minute Vocal Warm-Up

Have you noticed any improvement in your vocal skills after practicing the exercises given above? If you've followed the instructions closely, you're already developing a more flexible and dynamic speaking voice—an absolutely key skill for any good communicator and one that will add tremendously to your confidence.

Far more than any other asset you own, your voice is a *responsive* tool, only awaiting your skill in using it. Don't worry if you don't hear your voice responding in immediately dramatic ways. You've spent years developing your vocal habits, and it will take time to fashion your voice into a devastating delivery vehicle. But keep at it, and the progress you make will eventually surprise and delight you.

It's somewhere around that point in your personal development that someone will say to you: "That was a great presentation. Have you had voice training?" or "Have you been working with a speech coach?"

It's Time to Use Your Voice for Coloration and Effect. Now that you understand how your voice can affect others' receptivity of you and their perception of your message, you can use your vocal instrument to achieve a wide range of colorations and effects. Another way to say that is, your voice can now help you succeed at your *intentions* with this audience or individual listener.

For instance, you can sound somber or light-hearted if that's the effect you want at the moment. Or you can sound cajoling or compelling; skeptical or inspirational; doubtful or passionately persuasive; conciliatory or demanding. *By linking your intentions with your delivery skills, you can employ your full vocal range and virtuosity to drive home your critical messages and get listeners on board.*

One more point you should consider: vocal production is a *physical process.* Just as with any other muscle group, the vocal cords need to be warmed up to perform at their best. But with today's hectic professional schedules, getting in an adequate workout can be a challenge.

The solution is a vocal warm-up that takes just three minutes. Here is one that covers the following trio of essential areas (and it should be done in this order):

1. Breathing and resonance;
2. Supporting the sound; and
3. Warming up the articulators.

Here it is on the following page.

Step One:
BREATHING AND RESONANCE

- Stand comfortably with your feet at armpit width apart. Close your eyes. Take 3 slow, deep breaths. Imagine your breath as both nourishment and relaxing energy.

- Focus on your abdominal area. Feel your belly come out at inhalation, and go back in when you exhale. As you now know, this is healthy controlled breathing: diaphragmatic or *natural* breathing.

Step Two:
SUPPORTING AND SUSTAINING THE SOUND

- Breathe in slowly through your mouth to a silent count of 5. Retain the breath for a silent count of 5; then exhale gently to a silent count of 5. Do this 5 times.

- Choosing a comfortable pitch, produce the sustained sound "ahh." You should produce this sound quietly and gently, without attacking the vowel. At the same time, thinking of "placing" the sound at a spot 5 to 10 feet away from you—as though you were painting a dab of sound with a paintbrush on say, that clock on the wall. Don't "slide" up to the note. You're striking a balance: not getting up to the note sloppily, but not attacking it by making the sound harsh.

Step Three:
WARMING UP THE ARTICULATORS

- Below are some fun selections to further warm up those *articulators*: your lips, tongue, inside of your cheeks, and facial muscles. The pieces below are "patter songs" from 19th century Gilbert and Sullivan operettas: the absolute challenge for using rapid, crisp articulation. Use these selections, or tongue twisters, or anything similarly challenging as the last step before you speak. Your diction will then be sharp and clear!

From Gilbert and Sullivan's *Trial by Jury:*

When I, good friends, was called to the bar
I'd an appetite fresh and hearty.
But I was, as many young barristers are
An impecunious party.
I'd a swallow-tail coat of a beautiful blue
And a brief which I bought of a booby;
A couple of shirts, and a collar or two
And a ring that looked like a ruby.

At Westminster Hall I danced a dance
Like a semi-despondent fury;
For I thought I never should hit on a chance
Of addressing a British jury.
But I soon got tired of third-class journeys
And dinners of bread and water;
So I fell in love with a rich attorney's
Elderly, ugly daughter.

The rich attorney, he jump'd with joy
And replied to my fond professions:
"You shall reap the reward of your pluck, my boy
At the Bailey and Middlesex Sessions.
You'll soon get used to her looks," said he
"And a very nice girl you will find her;
She may very well pass for forty-three
In the dusk, with a light behind her!"

From Gilbert and Sullivan's *Iolanthe:*

When you're lying awake
With a dismal headache,
And repose is tabooed by anxiety,
I conceive you may use
Any language you choose
To indulge in, without impropriety;

For your brain is on fire,
And the bedclothes conspire
Of your usual slumber to plunder you:
First your counterpane goes,
And uncovers your toes,
And your sheet slips demurely from under you;

Then the blanketing tickles,
You feel like mixed pickles,
So terribly sharp is the pricking,
And you're hot, and you're cross,
And you tumble and toss
Till there's nothing 'twixt you and the ticking.

Then the bedclothes all creep
To the ground in a heap,
And you pick 'em all up in a tangle;
Next your pillow resigns
And politely declines
To remain at its usual angle!

Well, you get some repose
In the form of a doze,
With hot eye-balls and head ever aching.
But your slumbering teems
With such horrible dreams
That you'd very much better be waking.

And this famous selection from the same duo's
The Pirates of Penzance:

I am the very model of a modern Major-General,
I've information vegetable*, animal, and mineral,
I know the kings of England, and I quote the fights
  historical
From Marathon to Waterloo, in order categorical;
I'm very well acquainted, too, with matters
  mathematical,
I understand equations, both the simple and
  quadratical,

About binomial theorem I'm teeming with a
  lot o' news,
With many cheerful facts about the square of the
  hypotenuse.

I'm very good at integral and differential calculus;
I know the scientific names of beings animalculous:
In short, in matters vegetable, animal, and mineral, ,
I am the very model of a modern Major-General.

* That's pronounced with four syllables, "VEG-E-TA-BLE," to keep the scansion or meter of the verse.

Exercise 57: The Secret Strategy That Will Make What You Say Powerful

Do you think formal speeches are the occasions when you'll have maximum impact? And do you consider the data you're sharing to be the ultimate persuader?

If you answered yes both times, there's a technique you need to know about that should make your confidence soar—one which very few people are familiar with. It's a simple technique, yet one that can transform your ability to engage and move listeners. It's not only custom-made for the age we live in—it's also a central component to speaking with influence (and always has been). And it's just as dynamic for interpersonal communication as it is for speaking effectively as a professional.

I'm talking about *SPEAKING VISUALLY*—whatever your topic. In particular, I mean the ability to 'create word-pictures' in your audience's mind. Do so, and you'll allow each person to respond individually to what you're saying. In that way, they will have a reaction that's unique to them and thereby experience a stronger emotional response.

Any tool that does all that is one you need to use to become a powerful and supremely confident speaker!

Here's how it works, and the ways you can tap into and use this communication strategy to succeed when speaking to others.

YOU NEED TO PAINT WORD-PICTURES IN THIS VISUAL AGE

The greatest persuaders in the world today are television and the digital world of the Internet, smartphones, video games, etc. What's unique about them? They are mostly (sometimes completely) *visual.*

Over the past 75 years, these technological advances have fundamentally transformed how we receive and process information. Rather than reading or hearing material that we then agree or disagree with while forming mental images of our own, our lives have become a constant here-and-now at an entirely new level. But it's the *imagery*—in television broadcasts and online videos or interviews—that gives the information we receive maximum visceral impact.

The implication for effective business communication and interpersonal speaking is obvious, and here it is:

> To achieve effective communications in the 21st century, *you have to incorporate a strong* VISUAL COMPONENT *to accompany your words.* (And I've just done it right here, haven't I?)

Here's another fact concerning digitized information: Audiences now think in the microsecond rhythms of digital delivery. Watch a 1960's television drama and you'll wonder how anyone could have endured such a slow unwinding of the plot. So for improved public speaking in the 2000s, you need to speak visually, and you'd better be brisk about it.)

Creating 'Word-Picture' By What You Say. The most important need in this regard, however, is for you to employ visuals—for these days, that's how people learn. I'm not talking about flip-charts, PowerPoint slides, spreadsheets and other handouts, demonstration models, etc. I'm referring to creating 'word-pictures' by what you *say*.

You do this by investing whatever it is you're talking about—an event, feeling, emotion, story, plan or vision—with a rich enough description incorporating visuals that it comes to life in visceral and personal terms for listeners.

Let's say you're relating a visit you took to an outdoor market in, say, Lima, when you were visiting Peru to attend a conference. Well, you could say just that, couldn't you? —"We visited the famous Inka Market, an artisan market in the neighborhood of Miraflores. We saw all kinds of things being displayed for sale in terms of textiles, clothing, and jewelry." But how can that compare with this? — "We had some free time, so we visited the famous Inka Market—which is known worldwide for its high-quality artisan goods. What an explosion of the indigenous culture we saw on display! We walked past row after row of handmade clothing in vibrant local patterns, tables with brightly painted ceramics, and an explosion of alpaca scarves in every color you could imagine. It was all vivid, original, and striking. For a few minutes, I felt like I was really experiencing Peru in all its originality!"

Obviously, as you create these 'word pictures,' everyone in your audience will *see* these things in their mind's eye. Best of all, what they see is personal, since they will use similar things they've seen in their own lives to color the world you're creating for them now.

Getting the picture?

TAPPING INTO THE POWER OF VISUAL LEARNING

The visual aids I mentioned earlier (PowerPoint, flip chart, etc.), are still primary and useful. But there are two other powerful visuals you need to consciously use. Together, they should be part of your speaking strategy to make what you say have maximum impact.

The Visual You. The first is so close you may not be seeing it. It's *you*. That is, *the visual you.* You may employ visual aids when you need them. But you are the walking-talking visual, the one that is always "on."

Not only is your body an essential tool for amplifying and strengthening the points you're making. Equally important, what you show audiences in terms of body language, facial expressions, movement, and your willingness to get close to them, strongly affects others' ideas on how you feel about yourself and them. And that, of course, colors how they feel about you.

Your Second Secret Visual Tool. Your second powerful visual tool is STORYTELLING. All stories offer rich possibilities to use the visual elements today's audiences crave. They present the perfect opportunity to speak in visual terms, since they unfold as a series of pictures in listeners' minds.

Good speakers, in other words, know how to mimic a movie or TV show's visual unfolding of a story. At the start of World War II, when England faced Hitler's seemingly unstoppable German Army, the Wehrmacht, Winston Churchill might have stated flatly, "We will oppose the German invaders wherever they appear." Instead, this is what the British people heard him pledge on the wireless:

We shall fight on the beaches, we shall fight on the landing grounds, we shall fight in the fields and in the streets,
we shall fight in the hills; we shall never surrender.

Can't you see the fights going on in all those places had there
been a German invasion of England during the war?

HOW PEOPLE RESPOND TO VISUAL INPUT

You don't need to be Winston Churchill to tap into the power
and immediacy of speaking visually. Research has consistently
shown that people learn better, and retain information for longer
periods, when what they experience is presented visually.

A piece in *Psychology Today*, for instance, reminds us that a
much larger area of the brain is dedicated to processing visual
information over verbal input. Words, after all, are abstract,
whereas visuals are concrete. (Once, following one of my Public
Speaking class lectures at Tufts University where I mentioned
the need to be concrete in what you're presenting, an engineer-
ing student gave his informative speech on concrete, which I
thought was clever.) We might even say that our brain is more
"image processor" than word processor.[7]

But it's the other phenomenon at work when listeners process
visual information that's vital for you as a speaker: it creates an
emotional response. When you say, "The look on the little girl's
face brought tears to my eyes," each individual sees something
different, based on their experiences and what they've seen in
the past. So that visual is highly individual and wrapped up in
an emotional response in the hearer.

When it comes to speaking, then, you have a choice. If you
speak visually, you'll elicit a reaction from listeners that is private,

intensely personal, and with the power to create a strong emotional response. Or you can ignore all of this and simply read out your data. Can you see the difference?

To sum up, if you can consciously 'paint word-pictures' for people—in conversations, remarks, and formal speeches—it's a strategy that will make what you say infinitely richer and more personal for those listeners. That should be a powerful confidence builder for you!

NOTES

1 Shakespeare's plays are always a delight to act in, because he's a genius at constructing dialogue that captures the personality of each individual character. In a way, one doesn't have to do much when acting Shakespeare except speak the lines he's given you!

2 Barack Obama, President of the United States of America, State of the Union Speech (January 27, 2010).

3 Hillary Clinton, Secretary of State, United States of America, "Remarks on Internet Freedom," Newseum, Washington, D.C. (January 21, 2010).

4 Muhtar Kent, President and CEO, The Coca-Cola Co., "Are We Ready for Tomorrow, Today?," Investor and Analyst Event, The World of Coca-Cola, Atlanta, GA (November 16, 2009).

5 Yael Averbuch, Midfielder, Sky Blue FC women's professional soccer team, "Love the Process," National Soccer Coaches Association of America Women's Soccer Breakfast, Philadelphia, PA (January 21, 2010). This excerpt and the previous excerpts are taken from Vital Speeches of the Day LXXVI No. 3 (March 2010): 98-127.

6 Here are the speeds at which the vocal folds vibrate:

   · 110 cycles per second or Hz (men) = lower pitch
   · 180 to 220 cycles per second (women) = medium pitch
   · 300 cycles per second (children) = higher pitch/higher voice

   "Understanding Voice Production," The Voice Foundation. https://voicefoundation.org/health-science/voice-disorders/anatomy-physiology-of-voice-production/understanding-voice-production/

7 Haig Kouyoumdjian, "Learning through Visuals," Psychology Today, July 20, 2012. https://www.psychologytoday.com/us/blog/get-psyched/201207/learning-through-visuals

Succeeding In Social and Business Situations

Exercise 58: Are You Being Narcissistic?

In Chapter 6, "Changing Your Negative Thinking," you learned about the "self-fulfilling prophecy." That means to dwell on an unpleasant or unwanted outcome so much that the dreaded event actually comes to pass. The chapter that followed had to do with using positive visualization instead to "create your own success" in social and business situations. The visualizations you practiced were designed to put you in the right frame of mind prior to attending or appearing at such events rather than focusing on your anxiety.

Now you'll go one important step further—to reduce your nervousness *while you're engaged in these situations*. The exercises in this chapter are specifically designed to address the self-consciousness that leads to feelings of exposure, nervousness, and even fear. Their goal is to bring you out of yourself so you're more comfortable in front of others. They will help you to become more *person or "other" centered* (rather than yourself).

It's a well-known concept that turning your attention to others' needs rather than your own helps you to come out of yourself and stop obsessing over your problems. It's also absolutely the mark of confident and influential speakers.

THE SELF-CONSCIOUS PRESENTER

If you suffer from social anxiety, it's most likely true that you deal with powerful feelings of self-consciousness while appearing before others. And no wonder! Facing groups small or large—and even individuals—armed only with one's personality and some data to influence people professionally is a level of exposure that would make virtually anybody uncomfortable.

To add a huge level of uncertainty to the equation, perhaps *you* aren't the one who's supposed to be delivering tomorrow's project update after all. But Aliyah is home with the flu, so you've been tapped to give the presentation. So, you've had to get up to speed really fast—*too fast*. Also, you're slated to go to dinner with the client team tonight, and you've never met any of them. (Not to mention that this team is from Saudi Arabia, Aliyah is a native Arab speaker, and you only know English.)

Of course a situation like this one is going to make you self-conscious and nervous!

And even though deep down you realize that the situation isn't dangerous in any fashion, it still *feels* that way. Once you're in the grip of performance anxiety, the realization of your own vulnerability can crowd out every other consideration—including what you're trying to achieve with listeners.

Is the Size of Your Audience a Problem? Sometimes the

sheer size of your audience is what's making you anxious. Like most people, you're probably at ease in fairly intimate settings, talking to individuals or small groups—your family, say, or your team at work. In these situations, it's almost as though you were sitting around a campfire telling stories, given your familiarity and the cohesion of the family or team. (In evolutionary terms, I believe that's exactly what we feel).

But let's face it: a big audience of strangers for a formal speech or presentation—or even being introduced to, say, a large client team you've never interacted with before—is another matter entirely. Even though such groups are often made up of the same people you talk to without any self-consciousness in smaller gatherings, the stakes are raised when either the audience size or your unfamiliarity with the people in it changes. An audience in an auditorium is a crowd of strangers, after all! In these situations, ancestral memory seems to kick in and you feel totally out of place: exposed, facing an assembly of human beings whose intentions are unclear. You're painfully aware of being in unfamiliar surroundings among people you may not recognize, and certainly don't know whether to trust.

And in a minute, they're all going to be listening to what you have to say to convince them of something.

It's a recipe for extreme self-consciousness. And the only thing that seems to matter is getting yourself out of the exposed (i.e., dangerous) situation as quickly as possible.

Obviously, you have to remedy this situation. You need a way to reduce your self-consciousness and your desire for escape, and to bring your focus back where it needs to be. You find yourself grappling with a personality trait that we all possess to some extent, and which in this situation may be about to undermine your success.

That trait is *narcissism*.[1]

THE ISSUE OF UNINTENTIONAL NARCISSISM

This isn't to suggest that you're like the media mogul who said a few years ago, "If I only had a little humility, I'd be perfect." And it's certainly not to say that the narcissism you experience when appearing before others reflects a *desire* on your part to be the center of attention. Those are more along the lines of a narcissistic personality disorder.

No, your extreme self-focus is more something you're forced to deal with than a choice you've made. Still, there's no getting around that your self-consciousness is reaching its peak at these times. Let's look at this apparent contradiction and how it plays out when you speak to others in a public or semi-public setting.

NARCISSISM AND YOU

Just coming to the conclusion I shared above wasn't easy or clear-cut for me. In fact, I took a chance, some years ago, concerning the people who came to me for help with performance anxiety. I gambled that they wouldn't mind if I told them they were acting like narcissists. That gamble paid off—many of them readily acknowledged they understood that that's what was going on (in part). Since then, discussing narcissism has become an essential tool in my work helping people overcome their fear of public appearances.

This wasn't a great insight on my part. It simply involved listening to what my clients were saying.

As I listened to these people talk about their anxious thoughts and behavior, it struck me that nearly every sentence I was hearing began the same way. Listen yourself to these people describe their experiences with stage fright, and you'll hear it too:

- "I could hear my voice shaking."
- "I thought I was going to go blank and forget my content."
- "I had a panic attack just before I got up to speak."
- "I lay awake for weeks worrying about that upcoming appearance."
- "I could feel the sweat break out as we went around the table introducing ourselves."
- "I wanted to run out of the room."
- "I couldn't see the people in the hotel ballroom—it was like I suddenly went blind!"

You noticed it, didn't you? — Every sentence began with the word "I"!

Where, I wondered, were the words indicating the people being addressed: "they," "them," or "their"…or even "we" or "our" to discuss what these speakers and their listeners were about to experience together?

It was suddenly crystal clear to me that the *audience*—the most important people in the room—was being left out of the picture entirely by these anxious presenters!

That's when I realized that those who suffer from extreme stage fright are—unintentionally—living in a world of narcissism. This valuable insight opened up profitable avenues to treat the problem.

I began with a simple visual comparison which I named "The Two Solar Systems." It's the next exercise.

Exercise 59: The Two Solar Systems

As I say, I call this exercise concerned with narcissism The Two Solar Systems. It's my attempt to make clear to anxious clients and you, the reader of this book, the reality and consequences of a self-centered approach to presenting oneself to the world.

I knew, of course, that people suffering from performance anxiety don't expect to be told that they're too wrapped up in themselves! Yet the link seemed so clear that I thought bringing it out in the open would be an important step toward self-awareness and recovery.

Here's the exercise.

- Visualize a children's book image of our solar system (like this one, above). In this version, however, instead of the sun being at the center, there's a star with the word ME visible on its surface. (Could it have been you who wrote that word on the star?) Revolving around this star is *the*

rest of our solar system. Oddly enough, however, the other planets aren't named—only the "Me" sun at the center seems to matter:

- Now imagine you're looking at an illustration of our actual solar system (reproduced again, below). The sun, the familiar planets, the asteroid belt between Mars and Jupiter, they're all there. The star of this solar system (the real one) extends its life-giving radiance to this tiny sector of the Milky Way, the way it always has. That means it sustains our beautiful blue-green planet: Earth. We don't need to label it, for we all know what it is: *Sol*, or our sun:

COMPARING THE TWO ILLUSTRATIONS

Let's compare the two illustrations: The first drawing with "ME" as the center of everything, versus the reality of our actual solar system with the sun and nine planets (as long as you're not biased against Pluto).

If the source of all light and the heavenly bodies that depend upon it for their existence can be compared with you appearing before an audience—which of these two systems occupies your mind as you speak before others?

THE ME UNIVERSE: If you exist in the ME universe, you place yourself at the center of everything. Whatever happens during your presentation or remarks, you observe it and analyze it *only as it relates to your experience.* Whether you feel comfortable or uncomfortable, focused or distracted, confident or in panic mode, you measure everything in terms of how you are feeling.

In a word, you are being narcissistic. This way of thinking is fine if you're truly an egotist. But if your goal is to influence your audience positively and give them something of value, it's not so "hot" (sorry!).

THE UNIVERSE OF SUCCESSFUL PROFESSIONAL COMMUNICATION: In this version, the *they* of your audience, of course, becomes the "sun," which is at the center of things, not you. How could it be otherwise? Whether you're having a conversation, giving an update, pitching business, discussing an issue with a colleague or your boss, or delivering a presentation, the people you're speaking to are the only reason you're participating in this situation at all!

Your job is to influence them positively strictly in terms of their need to hear what you have to say. (E.g., If you don't hand out the spreadsheet or project the slide with next year's budget, how are they going to understand the company's financials?) Achieving this influence in terms of *their* needs is, surely, the true measure of your success.

Are you listening, "ME"? Or am I talking to you?

Exercise 60: Circles of Energy and Engagement

In my acting training at the Webber Douglas Academy of Dramatic Art in London, we studied a concept known as the Three Circles. The concept is just as relevant to *your* interactions with others and your level of confidence while participating in them. That's because knowing how to move through the three circles allows you to connect with those you're dealing with more securely and knowledgeably.

It all has to do with your energy level—overall and vocal—concerning your ability to successfully reach and engage other people.

FIRST CIRCLE reflects an intimate relationship. This is the type of interaction that takes place between lovers, spouses, and often, parents and children (and sometimes siblings). The circle is very small: encompassing, say, just the two of you. Talking, body language (often touching), the private nature of the conversation itself, and the energy expended in terms of vocal projection, are all quite specific to this circle. "Pillow talk" is an example of this. You might even whisper when you're discussing something with someone you're extremely close to in First Circle. You can immediately see that this is not the appropriate relationship for you at the office or in job-related encounters.

SECOND CIRCLE *is* appropriate for many of these

encounters. It is the conversational or professional circle. This level of engagement may be somewhat intimate in some situations, but most of the time it is not. Think of it as interacting with a person or persons standing 6' or so from you as you converse with them. Many of your interactions at the office or otherwise in your professional capacity will take place in Second Circle.

Immediately (as compared with First Circle), your energy level must change. With each of the circles, your energy output extends from you *to encompass everyone you're interacting with*. No one can be left out of the circle of influence! In effect, you are "reaching out" to this person or these people—expending the physical and vocal energy sufficient to include them in your thoughts and efforts to effectively engage with them in terms of what you're saying.

First Circle interactions, because of the intimacy involved, are necessary small (in physical terms) and private (in intellectual and emotional terms) To function well in Second Circle, however, is to be entirely professional along with an undeniable level of interaction which has to be *very effective* in your ability to deal with others. It may even lead to people thinking of you as charismatic, or someone who is good at interacting with others.

THIRD CIRCLE is the public circle. Now, we're talking about groups and audiences—from your team sitting around a conference table, all the way up to a speaking slot at an annual meeting or national conference. Your circle now must be very large—specifically, *including you and the person farthest from you in the room or auditorium.* You must now send much more energy outward in order to encompass everyone present.[2]

This is a very real need in performance when you're speaking in public. A bit of it involves larger gestures, but equally important is using the entire space or stage to *look* interesting and to get closer to the different parts of your audience. You really have to think in terms of a considerable output of energy for this (few speakers do). That's because you want each person in your audience to feel as though you're talking directly to him or her, no matter how far away from you they are. Do you see how, in Third Circle, your sheer output of energy, body language, and a well-projected voice will make you a more powerful and interesting speaker—and how using the same energy and externalization in either of the other two circles of energy is inappropriate?

Speaking of vocal projection:
Projecting Your Voice Adequately. From British voice coach Patsy Rodenburg comes a vocal exercise that will teach you proper projection of your voice. "Proper" because the vocal energy you give out must cross the physical distance between you and your audience, while still projecting power, warmth, and immediacy. (Here's a visualization I like to use: think of speaking to every listener so that that person feels as though you're putting your arm around their shoulder and speaking one-on-one. Can that be done even though you're projecting your voice with considerable energy? Of course. Use the vocal tools given in Exercise 53 in Chapter 11, especially changing the *vocal quality* of your sound.)

Here's Patsy Rodenburg's exercise[3] for voice projection:

1. Stand centered.

2. Put a hand about 9" in front of your face. Look at the hand and breathe to it. "Touch" and reach that hand with your breath.

3. Now put your hand down and focus on a point across the room. Breathe to *that* point. The breath has changed, expanded—you have to take more breath to reach that point.

4. Now extend yourself further. Imagine the whole room. Breathe to fill it. Notice the change of breath.

5. Finally, look out of a window and focus on a distant point, breathing to reach it. The greater the distance, the greater the breath needed to do so.

You shouldn't be surprised at this point to realize that to create greater energy to project your voice in a large space, the process starts with *breathing*. Remember, the greater the column of exhaled air that rises in your throat, the more the vocal folds are activated, producing larger sound waves that carry farther. In this case, it's simple physics. (It also teaches you not to try to "get louder" in your throat, which just strains the vocal folds. Keep your throat open and push out that wonderful volume of air you have from breathing diaphragmatically!)

Through the use of the three circles, you are now working consciously with physical expression and energy. From the audience's point of view, but also your own, you are demonstrating a *living*, more powerful presence through your conscious use of energy.

Welcome to more powerful, dynamic, and organic public speaking.

That thought should make you more confident!

Exercise 61: Entering a Room

This exercise might surprise you. A lot. I've seen it again and again over the years: people can really be astounded at how they're coming across to others.

That's what "Entering a Room" is all about finding out. I often use it when I'm conducting group training of a team, the C-suite of a company, the sales group, etc. The exercise has to do with physical expression—in this case, the impression others are gaining about you based on everything you're showing and the way you look and sound when you speak in public.

Here's how it works:

As long as the group or team I'm training isn't too large (5-8 people is ideal), I conduct this exercise at the beginning of our day-long workshop. I tell everyone that I'm going to give them a very short message to convey to the others in the group (who for this exercise will pretend they're the whole department, company, etc., whatever is appropriate).

One at a time, each person in turn will leave the room and close the door. A few seconds later, they will open the door and reenter, crossing to front-and-center. Then that person will say this:

"Good morning, everyone. Thank you for coming this morning. I have something of importance I'd like to say to you."

Everyone else then writes ONE WORD on a sheet of paper describing the feeling or "vibe" they're getting from the person in front of the room who just said that. The first person then sits down to join the others, and the next person takes their turn: leaving the room, reentering, crossing to the front of the room and saying exactly the same thing. We continue in this way until everyone has had a turn.

Then I ask each person to share out loud the word they wrote down for each speaker. Eventually, every participant has heard the single descriptive word their colleagues have used to describe them.

This is where the surprise—and sometimes the shock—comes in.

"Nervous." "Hurried." "Professional." "Angry." "Strict." "Tired." "Friendly." "Sweet." "Bossy." "Too serious." (Yes, people sometimes cheat and use more than one word—me too, as I also contribute my comments.) "Bad news." "Worried." "Easygoing." "Shy." "Introverted." (Or perhaps, "The company's about to be SOLD!")

Once we've heard everybody's opinion, and probably a few gasps, I ask: "So, what is the purpose to this exercise?

It isn't too hard, really. The point is *how much of the impression other people have of you depends solely upon nonverbal communication.* Everyone said exactly the same thing in front of the room, right? But the *physical* aspects of the moment: the way each person entered the room, held themselves as they walked to the front (slowly, deliberately, in a rushed fashion, looking like they were going to the electric chair?), made eye contact or not, displayed appropriate body language and any other signals—all of it was grist-for-the-mill in terms of people making judgments about that person.

Which, of course, they will also do with you in social and business situations!

I like the exercise because it goes straight to one of the primary purposes of my workshops. Specifically, it does a great job of showing: HOW MUCH OTHER FACTORS BESIDES YOUR CONTENT AFFECTS HOW YOU COME ACROSS TO PEOPLE AND HOW THEY RESPOND TO YOU.

And at some point, of course, I ask if anyone was surprised by the single descriptive word people gave them.

And boy, are some of them ever!

You can try this exercise with friends, colleagues, or teammates (I'd avoid family members). You needn't have everyone take a turn, unless they'd really like to find out what others think about *them*. But you can certainly go through it yourself to gain an idea from the others of the impressions you're broadcasting. Then you can ask yourself whether you want to do something about it. If you're shocked at what people are saying or you already know it's a problem for you, then you can consciously work on changing your body language and the overall physical expressiveness you're displaying in public.

Exercise 62: 10 Ways to Build Your Confidence in Social Situations

If you suffer from social anxiety, fear, or tend to dwell on negative self-talk when you're about to meet others—or all three—then social situations can be one of your biggest challenges. The threat you feel may be vague, i.e., a generalized social anxiety. Or it may be quite specific—your upcoming 360 performance review with your demanding boss, daily conversations you can't avoid with a difficult colleague, coordinating with another department that doesn't understand your team's responsibilities, or visiting a client firm that, like always, is going to expect the impossible.

In these situations especially, you need to build your confidence. The reason why, is that it directly impacts how others view you, how you view yourself, and how successful your interactions will turn out to be.

Below are 10 ways to achieve maximum presence and influence at these times. They are practical in nature and performance-oriented, having their roots in the theater where performing effectively is the name of the game. Therefore, they are simple tips which are easy to grasp and put into practice immediately, since *success in performance* is always an imperative of the stage. Together, they constitute a recipe for the type of success you need in social and business situations.

1. **Ground yourself.** As important as anything else going on at these moments, you want to have the sensation of being steady and secure. Start with feeling your feet gripping the floor. Imagine you've grown roots that go deep into the earth. The earth gives you energy and stability. You are steadfast and powerful! (Applies whether you're standing or sitting.)

2. **Exhibit good posture.** Again, standing or seated. *The way you hold yourself says much about how you see your place in the world.* It also makes a difference in terms of how strongly you and your ideas are accepted. And you will feel like you have a maximum of authority compared to slouching or being hunched over.

3. **Breathe deeply.** That, of course, means slow diaphragmatic breathing. As you've learned and practiced earlier in this book, "belly breathe" by taking full breaths. Then control your exhalation so you have something left when you reach the end of the idea where the important words reside. (Just like in that last sentence…"*where the important words reside.*")

4. **Dive into your audience.** Your audience is a pool. Don't back away from them, even if they're strangers. *Submerge* yourself in their energy and humanity. Relish the sheer reality of the current moment and the conversation you're having with them.

5. **Take…your…time.** Public speaking can make you speak too rapidly because of adrenaline, the "fight or flight" hormone. Take your time to cherish this opportunity, which is only here now and in a moment will be gone forever. Equally important, give your listeners time to absorb what you're saying before you go on to the next point. I almost never say to a client in a practice session: "Could you speak a little faster?"

6. **Pay attention with all of your senses.** Take in sensually everything that's going on around you. Hear with your eyes, feel the audience's reaction as if it were tactile; taste the ideas you're talking about in your mouth, etc. Respond with all your being! Remember my pencil exercise at the beginning of Chapter 5.

7. **Aim your energy outward.** Your audience matters, not you. (Remember: they are the sun in the solar system!) Don't give a thought to how you're doing. Instead, lose yourself in your message and how it is being received. If you are a leader who isn't used to hearing this, I will repeat it: you don't matter. Send the best of you to the people who do matter.

8. **Make eye contact as you tell the story.** The STORY is what the audience is here for. You can call it a narrative

or an update…or whatever. But you're always telling them a story of some kind. So, you're a storyteller. That means framing the narrative in terms of people. The rest of it—your data, sales figures, the challenges and triumphs your workforce faced, etc.—should be woven into the story of how a particular group of people (e.g., employees or customers) are affected.

9. **Trust silence.** Silence can be a thunderclap. It is therefore one of the most powerful tools in your public speaking toolbox. It helps you pace your presentation. It gives audiences time to fully grasp what you're saying. It builds up to dramatic revelations. Incidentally, it also tells audiences, "I'm confident enough to use silence for effect while I'm up here."

10. **Express yourself physically.** If you move while you speak, it will help you think and keep you in the moment. Strong, clean gestures amplify your content and bring it to life. The body is one of the primary tools of human communication, and ignoring it can turn you into a block of wood. If you're seated, simply use your arms, hands, upper body, face and eyes. *But give physical expression to the important things you say!* If you don't, we'll miss their immediacy and impact. We'll also miss the person behind the ideas, who formulated them and whom we're depending upon to lead us through their implementation.

Exercise 63: The Talk: "Tough Love"

You now have an idea from earlier in this chapter about the dangers of narcissism as you face fearful and anxiety-provoking situations. Let's go one step further concerning how you can become less self-centered in order to feed your own success as a professional.

First, a mini-review of that section of the chapter and the segment which followed. You learned about the link between narcissism and anxiety. You visualized the Two Solar Systems: one real, one ego-centered. And you read my message about turning your mind around so the audience rather than you is at center stage.

At this point, you're ready for some *tough love* concerning a non-narcissistic approach to facing your anxieties and fears. If you don't know the term, "tough love" means saying or doing something to someone you care about that may be painful for them but that is ultimately for their own good. So in that spirit, here are four tough-love messages that should help you overcome your extreme self-consciousness when dealing with others in important situations:

THE FOUR TOUGH-LOVE MESSAGES REGARDING YOUR APPEARANCES

1. **Get Over Yourself.** If the situation is, in fact, important, you must be focused on *contributing to its success* rather than how you yourself are doing. Yes, you deserve praise for participating and possibly speaking on the occasion (meeting, video conference, remarks at the annual meeting, whatever it may be) in spite of your apprehension and

self-perceived deficiencies. Still, you need to realize that *you're the least important person in the room.* Remember: the stakeholders are at the center of the entire communication process. You're there to reach out and benefit them, not to reach inward to yourself.

2. **It Ain't About You.** Anyway, what makes you think these attendees are here because of *you*? They're contributing their valuable time attending this event because they hope to get something out of it. Instead of being concerned about your own feelings, ask yourself if you're meeting their needs.

3. **People Don't Care About You.** That may sound harsh, but it's true. People are always in a "What's-in-it-for-me?" mode when they attend any event or meeting. They aren't paying any attention to (and many times, not even noticing) your nervousness or discomfort. And the odds are they don't care about your looks either. They're concerned instead with the information you're imparting, whether it will help them in some way, and feeling that their time being here has been well spent. This reminder that they're not paying that much attention to you personally is GOOD NEWS!

4. **Be Professional.** You have a professional responsibility—a fiduciary duty—to do your job in this situation. So play the role assigned to you. It's what you're being paid for, isn't it, or at least what you're receiving recognition and credit for? So shut up and do it!

Told you it was tough love!

Anyway...lecture over. Kindly have the car keys back by 11 p.m.

Love, Dad.

Exercise 64: 10 Fast and Effective Ways to Overcome Stage Fright

Let's talk about stage fright.

Chances are that as a professional, a significant part of your job involves speaking publicly. That definition may include:

- Contributing to weekly team meetings.
- Giving project updates.
- Presenting monthly to your department or leadership team.
- Giving presentations at video conferences.
- Contributing to organizational decisions.
- Training or orienting new employees.
- Pitching business.
- Speaking regularly to (and visiting) clients and customers.
- Meeting deadlines and quotas.
- Taping video clips or podcasts (internally or for external use).
- Delivering a keynote address.
- Attending annual meetings and user conferences.
- Participating in panel discussions.
- Being interviewed on stage, or on a TV news or business show.

- Holding a press conference or crisis conference.
- Testifying before regulatory bodies.

That's a lot of opportunities for anxiety and revisiting your fears, worrying about exposure, reembracing the Imposter Syndrome, or relapsing into negative thinking. And given the pressure (or panic!) involved, these appearances can make it impossible to be "in the moment." When you're facing a large audience that's testing your confidence, you may just be hoping to get through your presentation as quickly as possible to get it over with!

Obviously, speech anxiety and stage fright are limiting your peace of mind in these situations.

Twenty-two million Americans. That's an estimate of the number of people in this country who suffer from fear of public speaking. That figure represents a percentage of the 70-75 percent of people surveyed who report some level of glossophobia or speaking apprehension.[4]

That's twenty-two *million*. And then there's the rest of the world. If you're a member of that congregation, wouldn't you appreciate learning how to love public speaking instead?

10 HELPFUL WAYS TO DEAL WITH FEAR OF PUBLIC SPEAKING

Learning to love speaking in public may seem like a distant goal to you at this point. But it's actually closer than you think. As a first step, remind yourself that the topic you're passionate about is most likely also of interest to listeners. And they *are* listening, not thinking about you and your nerves (or even your speaking skills).

Here are 10 "quick fixes" that you can use for even more practical approaches to be at your best when stage fright comes to call.

1. **Get Your Head In The Right Place.** I'm going to start out with one of my tough love messages: It ain't about you! Speech anxiety is unpleasant enough if you focus on how awful you're feeling instead of what really matters: the response of your audience. Put yourself in their shoes and think about what they're hoping to get out of this presentation. You'll quickly get yourself on the right wavelength, which is that of your audience.

2. **Belly Breathe.** Modern life with all its gadgets and digital assistants makes it easy for you to become a "talking head," which includes breathing shallowly and rapidly into speech aids like cell phones and microphones. The fight-or-flight response to social anxiety exacerbates this type of respiration cycle. To counter these habits, learn how to breathe diaphragmatically (review Chapter 2 on breathing techniques). Yes, it will help you to have a more pleasant and resonant voice. But more importantly if you're anxious and nervous, it will calm you and slow your heart rate.

3. **Turn That Negative Talk Into Positive Thinking.** The longer you stay in negative territory concerning your response to public speaking, the more it will seem like home. We're all experts at beating ourselves up through negative self-talk. And the brain learns from negative thinking so that it becomes more efficient in making that outcome happen! Why not spend your time usefully and employ positive thinking instead? Turn self-destructive

statements into self-fulfilling prophecies of success (see "the brain learns" just above). Flip your negative mindset. Create a positive groove so that speaking opportunities turn out to be not only more successful but enjoyable.

4. **Stand Straight and Open Up Your Chest.** Body language matters in terms of how confident you look! Try this: hunch your shoulders slightly. Now instead, stand straight, allowing your chest area to come forward as your shoulders drop into their natural position. Breathe deeply. Doesn't making this simple change make you feel more confident? You certainly will look more professional, and sure of yourself!

5. **Let Go Of Intrusive Thoughts.** Focus is one of your most important tools when it comes to reaching and engaging audiences. But you're human, which means off-the-grid thoughts will intrude when you don't want them to. (Remember the Actor's Box exercise in Chapter 7?) Learn not to engage these thoughts or resist them either. Instead, simply notice them then let them float away! Come back to your message and whether it's being received by listeners.

6. **Greet Your Audience And Smile.** One of the most effective ways to have a relationship with an audience is to take a moment to allow that to happen. You do that in your GREETING. Presenters are always super-focused on the content of their speeches and presentations, but hardly ever take a moment to greet their listeners and start the journey together. Be sure to include a greeting. And really

invest yourself in this moment, letting listeners know that you truly enjoy the opportunity to speak to them. Presenters say all the time, "Thank you for having me. It's a pleasure to be here at the conference," and never sound like they really mean it. If you mean it, allow listeners to hear the emotion in your voice. Interestingly, you too will feel it when you HEAR yourself speak that way!

7. **Don't 'Present'…Have A Conversation.** Edward Everett was a famous nineteenth century orator. In fact, he was chosen to deliver the keynote address at the dedication of the Union cemetery at Gettysburg on November 19, 1863. But we remember the other guy—the fellow named Abraham Lincoln who gave the two-minute speech after Mr. Everett's two-hour oration. And it was that concise conversation with the audience—Lincoln's—that came to be known as America's most famous speech, the Gettysburg Address.

"Orations," as they were known at the time, were apt to go on for hours, *with every word memorized by the orator.* With each decade that has passed since then, however, public and private speeches have been getting more and more colloquial and informal-sounding.

Okay, you're probably not delivering a national address. But that fact should only help you become less formal-sounding and more conversational. One way to do that is to STOP THINKING OF WHAT YOU'RE DOING AS A SPEECH OR PRESENTATION AT ALL. You're no longer expected to have your finger poking holes in the air as you deliver your momentous oration.

It's just a *conversation* now—as though you were speaking to these people in your living room. Doesn't that sound like an easier and more enjoyable task than thinking of yourself as being center stage in front of all these people and having to be *good*?

Try thinking of your talks that way!

8. **Visualize A Successful Outcome.** Athletes, chess players, and golfers use positive visualization to "see" what may unfold before they get to that moment. You should too. In other words, help yourself create a successful presentation! It just makes sense: the more time and effort you spend anticipating positive outcomes, the better prepared you'll be to respond that way in the real situation.

9. **Turn The Spotlight Around.** Speaking in public can feel like standing alone in a hot bright spotlight. There, every move you make is visible to everyone, and can make you feel naked and vulnerable. So, here's another visualization technique. Turn that spotlight around. Now, you're in the cool dark and the spotlight is shining brightly on the audience. As I said elsewhere in this book, aren't you supposed to "illuminate" your listeners?

10. **Move!** Ever feel like you're in a pressure cooker when speaking to a group? With the fight-or-flight response comes the release of stress hormones that are telling you to do battle with the threat or escape as fast as you can. If you stand or sit stock-still, the pressure will just build.

So, move! You'll feel released; and even small movements use up some of the adrenaline that's now infusing your muscles, trying to get you to act! You'll also feel more like yourself if you can move and gesture naturally. There are always excuses to move: to point something out on the screen with your slide deck, to approach an audience member who has just asked a question as you begin your answer, or just to get closer to the audience when you want to share something important with them (an actor's trick you should remember—it's called "going center-stage" or "down-center"). Movement is entirely natural in an energized and passionate speaker, and when it isn't there, we wonder why.

Exercise 65: Seven Tips for a Successful Job Interview

As you know, or should know, a successful job search is only partly about the knowledge and experience you display in the interview itself. Other behaviors that you exhibit can also be part of whether you find success. These include your phone skills in setting up the interview; the way you treat subordinates (I've seen a situation where this made a difference in the hiring executive's opinion of the candidate, who had been officious and condescending to the receptionist); your ability to converse naturally in the interview; your prompt and professional follow-up to the meeting; any personal connections that can bolster your candidacy; a special interest in the company that you can give evidence of, and so on.

That said, your interaction with your interviewer(s) or hiring committee remains the single most important factor in landing a position. Here are seven tips for standing out from the crowd as you seek that dream job:

Tip #1: Show initiative and confidence. Your interviewers have brought you in because they genuinely want to know who you are and how you might fit into their organization. They'll have a hard time figuring any of this out if you sit blandly, responding robot-like to their questions.

Have the confidence and courage to be you. That means taking your responses into your home territory, not merely following the crumbs to where you think they want you to go. Your interviewers know you're probably nervous. (Sometimes they're nervous themselves.) Exhibiting sufficient self-esteem will differentiate you from all the other candidates who come across as *just* nervous. (Remind yourself of Exercise 47 in Chapter 10 on body language and nonverbal communication: "Fake-It-Till-You-Make-It: How To Broadcast Confidence (Even If You're Not Feeling Any)."

Tip #2: Take the first step. When you walk into your interviewer's office, be the one to initiate the moment of greeting: "So nice to meet you. Thank you for having me here today," is a simple yet great opener. Do you have a mutual acquaintance or share a hobby? Mention it! Showing enough initiative to reach out first is a very good sign. So, act rather than react.

Tip #3: Notice, and comment. What is there in the room or environment that you can comment on? Is the view from the wall of windows stunning? (Many of the office towers in Boston's Financial District offer a gorgeous view of Boston Harbor, the harbor islands, and Logan Airport.) What about that intriguing Balinese mask on the wall? What's that ancient baseball glove signify—did this person play professional baseball at some point? I remember an interview where the person interviewing me had on display an Olympic silver medal. You can bet I asked about that! And, yes, he'd won it at an Olympics many years earlier.

Remember: most applicants arrive, sit down, and begin answering questions. What's memorable about that? *Where's the human being, apart from the financial analyst or recent law graduate they invited to interview for the job?* Believe me, if you make an intelligent and unexpected (and appropriate) comment to start out, you'll be remembered. Take a seat only once you're invited to, and keep in mind the following points as you speak.

Tip #4: Display your mind's organization and use of logic. Go beyond the bare answer to questions that allow only a cut-and-dried response. Show that you've invested some thought in this industry and this company in particular, and your possible place in the scheme of things. Try to make it appear that you're a self-starter with a nimble mind. *And look for ways to include the position and/or company's name (say it) in some of your answers.* (Obviously, don't overdo it.)

For instance, when I'm coaching executives for a job interview they have coming up, I remind them not just to say something like, "And that project was when I learned how to _____ ." Instead, why not make it: "And that project was when I learned how to _____, which I think is an invaluable skill I'll use in the position here at The Sky's the Limit Investments."

Make your points as concisely and crisply as you can, *and back each one up with evidence.* This can include customer testimonials, data you're familiar with, recent studies, government statistics or industry news, well-known business outcomes, and of course your personal experiences with the matter at hand. These and other forms of evidence elevate what you just said from being merely your opinion.

Be firm without being dogmatic, generous when mentioning others, personable but not silly. Impress them with the value of your opinions, without seeming to consider them worthy of Fort Knox. Some of the questions you're asked will be designed not to test your knowledge (there may not BE any hard-and-fast data to point to), but to see if you have an organized and logical mind. After all, if you get the job, problems will arise that no one will have foreseen, and your ability to find a solution using that keen mind of yours is something the company will be interested in.

Tip #5: Be enthusiastic! Convey the impression that this employment opportunity doesn't just interest you—it *excites* you. Be honest, though. Avoid coming across as a wide-eyed innocent who is, golly, just thrilled at the possibility of working *at this magnificent firm.* But be enthusiastic enough (if you honesty are), so that the interviewers can pick up on your energy level and get a charge from it themselves. They'll feel good about the interview afterwards, even if they can't put their finger on exactly why.

Tip #6: Try your best to be human. That means showing emotions. Don't buy into the myth that emotions have no place in the world of business and the professions. And female executives: avoid trying to come across as masculine, including what you wear (you know, shades of male business suits). The interviewer(s) wants to see and hear you, not the cliché of the man-like businesswoman ready to start throwing her sharp elbows everywhere. We should be well and truly past that now. Everybody: be passionate about the things that matter to you (but don't come across as obsessive). Just be sure that your deeply held convictions are in line with their thinking and business practices.

Tip #7: Smile. You probably don't smile enough when you're under pressure. If this job interview appears to be making you work like hell, it'll seem like hard work for your interviewer too. He or she may even get the impression that the thought of being part of this organization is too difficult an undertaking for you. Instead of leading them to such a grim conclusion, try to seem like a pleasant person to be around.

Most of all, don't be a mysterious personage that needs information coaxed out of him or her, grunt by inconclusive response. That works for Hollywood anti-heroes and comic book crime-fighters, but not for gainfully employed professionals.

Bonus Tip #8: Not Caring. Does it help if, instead of going into a high-stakes interview with a load of trepidation on your shoulders, you tell yourself you really aren't too concerned whether you get the job or not? For some of my clients, this has been the case from time to time. It can visibly transform Herculean efforts to look and sound good (which can sometimes be obvious), and instead display a nonchalance that translates into...*confidence*. It can come across as: "I'm totally qualified and I think it would be interesting to work here—and to the company's advantage as well as my own. But if I don't get this gig, I'll get one somewhere else."

Be careful, though. We're not talking smug or conceited by any means. Do everything that's mentioned in the tips above. The difference will be in your mindset: that you're not putting such pressure on yourself. So, if you decide to try this way of thinking and you feel you can pull it off, I'll say this: Option A: Where the interviewer thinks, "This person is brilliant but relaxed. I like that." beats Option B, where he or she thinks, "This person obviously knows her stuff...but she seems so tense. I wonder why."

Just as in meetings and presentations, you never want your audience to stop thinking about the story you're telling them to wonder *what's going on with this person?*

NOTES

1   Do you know the origin of the term? Narcissus was a beautiful young man in Greek mythology who rejected all who loved him. As punishment, the gods made him fall in love with his own reflection in a forest pool, and he wasted away because he couldn't bear to leave that reflection. According to the myth, the narcissus flower grew up on that spot.

2   But what about virtual communication? You obviously can't expend enough physical energy to reach someone on the video call who is in, say, Singapore when you're in New York. We might, in fact, call this a Fourth Circle of energy, in which you teach yourself to project the energy of your personality and professionalism as it is perceived through the web-cam, which is your "projector" to reaching people worldwide. Pay attention to how people who are effective in video meetings manage it in terms of voice, body language, and especially, facial expressions when interacting with their web-cam. Though it may seem like a mysterious process at first, you'll pick it up quickly and get comfortable—and confident—in how it's done well.

3   Patsy Rodenburg, The Actor Speaks (New York: St. Martin's, 2000), 56.

4   Gary Genard, Fearless Speaking (Arlington, MA: Cedar & Maitland Press, 2014), 217, citing Karen Kangas Dwyer, Conquer Your Speechfright (Fort Worth: Harcourt Brace, 1998), 3-12, per McCroskey, 1993; and Richmond & McCroskey, 1995.

CHAPTER 13

Your Personal Brand

Exercise 66: Charisma vs. Authenticity

ON CHARISMA

So, what about the question of charisma? Doesn't coming across as a confident and magnetic personality mean that people should be fascinated with you from the get-go? And if so, where does that magic come from? Does *executive presence* to justify such confidence require any technique at all, or is it all just mystique?"[1]

If you're in the mystical camp—if you accept the definition of charisma as "a divinely conferred power or talent"[2]—you won't agree with Roger Ailes, who had this to say in his book *You Are the Message*:

'Charisma' is a powerful but often misunderstood word. It derives from the Greek *kharisma*, meaning favor or divine gift, and its root is *kharis*, meaning grace. The dictionary defines [it] as 'a special, inspiring quality of leadership.' It's really the ability to subtly cause others to react to *you* as opposed to your reacting to them. People with charisma seem to be in charge of their lives. They seem to have a goal, a purpose, a direction—in fact, a mission."[3]

Now, aren't the character traits of "being in charge of your life," and "having a goal and a purpose," within your grasp? Even if you're an extraordinary person who emits a special aura in front of others, you still have the task of meeting the needs of the people you're interacting with.

As my ideas and opinions in this book should have shown you by now, as a lifelong performer, I believe that having a goal and a purpose, and *caring about audiences of stakeholders more than you care about your performance,* is all-important. Having that attitude seems to me to embody the type of behavior and actions that may very well lead to people finding you charismatic.

And if they don't think that, so what?

It's always more important to be responsible, honest, and sincerely out to help others in your dealings with them.

That's what you're there for.

And besides, when it comes to influencing listeners, that what moves the needle every time.

Exercise 67: Your Personal Brand Is Everything

In this exercise, I'd like to discuss an area that is increasingly important in 21st-century professional life. I'm referring to your personal brand.

Today, when it's possible through the internet to reach thousands or even millions of people through what you say, developing a personal brand is a powerful tool of influence. Your image among the people who see and hear you—whether it's in person, online, on video, or through podcasts—is a key element of your personal and professional persona and success.

If you can build your confidence *as you display and live your brand*, there are very few limits as to what you can achieve.

In other words, shaping and strengthening your brand is a vital tool of personal empowerment. Of course, this means you need to be exceptionally good at showcasing your brand whenever you present yourself.

In the past, your impact was limited to the people sitting in an audience, along with those in your industry who heard about you, and perhaps, people who saw you in the local media. But as public relations specialist Richard Dowis has said, today, "a speech can have a life far beyond the twenty or thirty minutes [you] spend in delivering it."[4]

THE SEVEN ESSENTIAL QUALITIES OF YOUR BRAND

How do you develop a brand? Like all true influence, the necessary starting place has three characteristics: honesty, authenticity, and the desire to give those you're interacting with what you think they need. (Notice that your needs don't show up in this equation.) Here are the qualities you should exemplify: (1) Integrity, (2) Passion, (3) Energy, (4) Goodwill, (5) Vulnerability[5], (6) Empathy, and (7) Humility.

Naturally, your performance skills matter as well, whether you're sharing data, giving your opinion, or taking center stage. If it's public speaking you're engaged in, remember that a speech or presentation is always a journey that the speaker and audience go on together. Therefore, your effectiveness goes far beyond content and expertise. It hinges upon whether the people in the room or auditorium are better off for your having had a conversation with to them.

It's all part of what I call *high-impact speaking*.

HOW ARE YOU PERFORMING YOUR LIFE?

At the very beginning of this book, I asked the question: *"Are you ready to show yourself to the world?"* You see, developing and living your brand goes deeper than doing well "in the moment" of your professional task, whatever it may be. It's part of the larger question of how you're "performing" your life where others are concerned (especially those you're trying to influence).

Part of the reason this is such an important concept is that people can only react to what you're showing them. That's true whether you're delivering a speech or chatting with a neighbor at the supermarket. People gain impressions of who you are not by conjuring those perceptions out of thin air, but because *you've given them something to perceive.* Audiences and other listeners can't read your mind to know how you really feel about what you're saying. The performance you broadcast is the one they will receive! It depends on connecting with people through the following tools, among others:

- Intensive and active listening.
- Your vocal approach.
- Body language and expressing yourself physically.
- Facial expressions.
- Eye contact.
- Achieving and demonstrating empathy.

- The rhythm and urgency of your speech.
- Your efforts of any kind to get closer to those you're talking to and to understand them better.

Audience and listener perceptions aren't casual matters, either. People are deciding whether they can trust you, whether you're knowledgeable about a topic, or if they should believe what you say. They are observing how you feel about *them*, and sometimes, your feelings toward yourself. If it's a business transaction, they are very definitely considering if they're willing to buy what you're selling, or whether they want to work with you.

You're Already a Natural. The good news is that you're already a natural at speaking to people about something you share an interest in with them. You not only already have all the tools you need to make these interactions successful and to instill trust in those listening to you, but you've been using them all your life. Your touchstone should therefore be this: answering affirmatively when you ask yourself, "Am I being honest in what I'm saying, and focused on *their* understanding of it?"

Tapping into these simple truths should give you a tremendous amount of confidence in your abilities. Too many people *try to be good in order to help themselves.* Helping others—since you are the one tapped to do it in these cases—is a much surer path to success.

And to greater confidence that you're the right one for the job.

Exercise 68: The Top 10 Causes of Communication Anxiety

How's this as an attention-grabber for your next presentation? — Speech anxiety ranks higher than death as the fear people mention most often!

To be fair: heights, insects, and deep water *also* rank above death in the survey that's still cited above any other. It's from *The Book of Lists,* which in 1977 reproduced a 1973 survey by Bruskin Associates. Here's the full ranking of the "14 worst human fears":

1. Speaking before a group
2. Heights
3. Insects and Bugs
4. Financial Problems
5. Deep Water.
6. Sickness
7. Death
8. Flying
9. Loneliness
10. Dogs
11. Driving in a Car
12. Darkness
13. Elevators.
14. Escalators.

To bring that up to date to our 21st century, a recent post from a "knowledge, awareness, and self-improvement" site finds fear of public speaking occupying the #3 slot these days. In this newer list, a dread of loneliness and death edge out our social phobia. But fear of speaking reliably remains an ongoing day-time nightmare.

That's why I wanted to include this exercise in the book, in case you're one of the many millions of people worldwide for whom *glossophobia* or fear of public speaking is chipping away at their confidence. Which is to say, if you fear speaking in public more than riding an escalator, you're certainly not alone. Speech jitters still ranks high the world over on lists of things people would rather not do if they can get out of it. But what specifically causes this type of social anxiety?

THE TOP 10 REASONS YOU HAVE STAGE FRIGHT

Here's what you need to know to start your journey to greater confidence and enjoyment of public speaking. Based on my career as an actor and 24 years as a speech coach, this is my take on the ten biggest reasons you have this fear. Also included are my tips on how you can overcome it...and basically get your life back!

1. **Self-consciousness in front of large groups.** This is the most frequently named reason for performance anxiety. Speech coaches often hear: "I'm fine talking to small groups, but when it's a large audience I get really anxious." Two strategies will help: (1) Remember that the people in a big audience are the same ones you talk to individually, and (2) Concentrate on just talking to them, not "presenting". You'll be at your best.

2. **Fear of appearing nervous.** Do you fear that you'll *look* fearful? Many speakers do. It's easy, then, to believe that if the audience sees those nerves, they'll think you don't know your topic. But of course the two aren't

linked. When you see that a speaker is nervous, don't you sympathize, rather than making a judgment on that person's professionalism? If anything, your audience will extend you sympathy not resistance.

3. **Concern that others are judging you.** The tough-love message here is that people really don't care about you. They're in the audience to get something out of your lecture, presentation, or speech. They want their time to be well spent. Watching a speaker fail is embarrassing for everyone. So the audience is actually pulling for you!

4. **Past failures.** Public speaking anxiety is often learned behavior. That is, at some point in the past you failed, and the seed of self-doubt was planted. But if you know your stuff and are prepared *this time*, there's no reason for things to go south like they did in the long ago. Not unless you insist that that's what will happen, and believe it. Plan to succeed instead.

5. **Poor or insufficient preparation.** See #4 above. If you haven't done your homework (including analyzing your audience to understand them and their needs), there's no reason you should succeed. Blame nobody but yourself. Nothing undermines public speaking confidence like being unprepared. But nothing gives you as much confidence as being ready. Your choice.

6. **Narcissism.** You remember Exercise 58, "Are You Being Narcissistic?" in Chapter 12, don't you? This is also related to the tough-love message I gave in Exercise 63, "The Talk: Tough Love." To repeat, indulging in extreme

self-consciousness while speaking is narcissistic. How can you influence others if you're totally wrapped up in yourself? You can't. So turn that bright spotlight around and "illuminate" your listeners. You don't matter. They do.

7. **Dissatisfaction with your abilities.** Okay, this is a legitimate concern. But it's also one of the easiest of my Top 10 causes to remedy. You *should* feel dissatisfied if your speaking skills are below par. But dissatisfaction can be an excellent spur. Get the speech training you've been thinking about. Just knowing you have first-rate skills can provide you with a truckload of confidence. It's also much more likely to make you eager to speak.

8. **Discomfort with your own body.** Why is it that we're all at ease physically with friends, but self-conscious and awkward in front of an audience? If that's you, re-read the tips I give elsewhere in these pages about having a conversation with listeners. That should help you relax into your body. Also, pay attention to how you stand, sit, gesture, and move when you're in a comfortable environment. Then recreate that natural movement with larger (and more formal) audiences.

9. **Poor breathing habits.** Unless you've been trained as an actor or classical singer, you're probably unaware of how to breathe for speech. Public speaking requires more air than "vegetative breathing." Also, you need to control your exhalation to sustain sound through the end of your expressed idea (*that* I mentioned previously as well). As you already know, diaphragmatic breathing

is the way to do all of this. It's also great for calming your galloping heart.

10. **Comparing yourself to others.** Don't do it! Your job is never to be an "excellent" speaker. It's to be interesting when you discuss your topic or passion. That's it. The really good news is that no one in the entire universe can do that as well as you, because you're the person to tell us about it. Truly, you're the one we came to hear.

Exercise 69: How to Get People to Trust You

I'm betting that in addition to your wanting to boost your confidence and reduce your fears and anxieties, you would like to be seen as good at what you do—perhaps even exceptional. Yes?

To do that, you need to be willing to go beyond the technical aspects of your job. This is the problem faced by people who excel at positions that are basically technical (or data-driven in nature), who are *so* good at it that they get promoted. Now that they are a manager or team leader or director, they realize that *managing people* is a core element of their job. In other words, they now need to go far beyond the technical/analytical/data-centered expertise that got them to this point, and quickly learn about managing those reporting to them.

All while communicating effectively in the other direction as well: with their boss, and with divisional and company leaders.

If this is the case—or becomes the case—with you, there are some more subtle aspects of a winning communication style you should be aware of. Among them are speaking with simplicity and clarity in a conversational tone, and being seen as likable.

(To tease out that third one a bit, some executives realize that their too-brash—or two quiet—a speaking style is anything *but* conversational, and it's undermining their authority. That's when some of them seek out a speech coach.)

As a speaker, you should always try to speak simply and clearly. One of history's most creative thinkers, Leonardo da Vinci, said, "Simplicity is the ultimate sophistication." Some of the most famous speakers in our language left an historical legacy because plain speaking rings throughout their phrases. Here are some examples:

- Abraham Lincoln's "government of the people, by the people, for the people."

- Winston Churchill's "never in the field of human conflict was so much owed by so many to so few."

- Martin Luther King, Jr.'s "I have a dream."

- Sojourner Truth's "Ain't I a Woman?"

- Ronald Reagan: "Mr. Gorbachev, tear down this wall!"

- George W. Bush, in a bullhorn address to Ground Zero rescue workers after 9/11, when some workers shouted: "We can't hear you!" responded this way: "I can hear you! I can hear you! The rest of the world hears you! And the people—and the people who knocked these buildings down will hear all of us soon!"

Anglo-Saxon over Latin. Whenever you speak, whether it's in a simple conversation to a formal presentation, it's always true that 'nickel' (simple) words land with more impact than 'dollar' (sophisticated) words. In our language, much of this has to do with the hard-hitting quality of *Anglo-Saxon* versus *Latin's* more ornate approach. For example "chew" is simple Anglo-Saxon, the more sophisticated "masticate" is Latin. Increasingly in our culture and language, the greatest thoughts are expressed as simply as possible, because simple language can be understood by everyone.

Consider this excerpt that shows the power of simple language. Richard Dowis wrote it:

> Short words can make us feel good. They can run and jump and dance and soar high in the clouds. They can kill the chill of a cold night and help us keep our cool on a hot day. They fill our hearts with joy, but they can bring tears to our eyes as well. A short word can be soft or strong. It can sting like a bee or sing like a lark. Small words of love can move us, charm us, lull us to sleep. Short words give us light and hope and peace and love and health— and a lot more good things. A small word can be as sweet as the taste of a ripe pear, or tart like plum jam. Small words make us think. In fact, they are the heart and soul of clear thought.[6]

Did you notice that this entire 141-word passage consists of only one-syllable words?

HAVE A CONVERSATION WITH LISTENERS

If you want people to trust you—and as I've said before in this book—have a *conversation* with them, using the simplest and clearest words possible. In fact, it's when your words are simple and clear that you're actually having a *conversation* with your listener(s)—whether it's one person or a thousand—rather than talking at them. That's a key to influential speaking. Why? Because both you and listeners are at your best when you are conversing with each other. That's when both sides are most natural and least self-conscious. Isn't the thought of having a conversation with someone less intimidating to you than an upcoming speech?

The Advantage of Conversations. Because you're at ease in a conversation, you look and sound more like yourself. You gesture and color your voice in a way that's much closer to the real you than during "public speaking" or "presenting." You're relaxed, and it shows—so you're much better at expressing genuine passion and empathy. Any audience hearing you in that vein will relax into the conversation, becoming more open and receptive. Why wouldn't they? If you're genuinely enthused about your topic, you'll be more enjoyable to listen to than if you're trying to be a good speaker.

CAN YOU 'CHAT' ABOUT IMPORTANT TOPICS?

There's another reason being conversational is vital to speaking today. Television—and now videoconferences—have changed the game. TV started it all by bringing people into everyone's living room. Suddenly, performers weren't speaking from public stages with us in the audience. From news anchors to game show hosts, they were *in our homes*. And they became very good at being conversational—at just *chatting* with us—because their performance demanded it. Mass communication became closer and warmer and more casual than it had ever been before.

These days, experts and everyday people alike often chat with us via Zoom meetings, webinars, podcasts, and FaceTime. We even see them fumbling to press the right button to get things started…why, they're just like us!

The result is that more than ever we expect speakers to be conversational, even about important issues. Watch a video of John F. Kennedy's inaugural speech from 1961 and compare it with a speech on the same occasion by any of our recent presidents. You may be struck by how far we've come toward conversational public speaking, even in highly formal settings. To connect with listeners—no matter your topic or profile—you must strike a balance between professionalism and having a conversation with those listening.

A MAGIC BULLET OF SPEAKING SUCCESS: LIKABILITY

And it's important to be likable too. The speech coach to President Ronald Reagan (who possessed some charm as a speaker) called likability a "magic bullet," and considered it a critical factor in speaking success. "If your audience likes you," he said, "they'll forgive just about everything else you do. If they don't like you, you can hit every rule right on target and it doesn't matter."[7]

Getting to Memorability and Trust. Get an audience to like you, and they will more likely enjoy being in your company. Many business presenters keep their distance from the audience because they're more attuned to their content than to listeners. You need to go in exactly the opposite direction. If it's clear to people that you care deeply whether they understand—and if you're working at establishing a relationship with them—they'll sense something happening in the room. It will seem to them like a shared experience. And indeed, it will be. They'll think of this speech as something memorable. If that happens, it's guaranteed that they will think the same of you.

Just as important, they will be much closer to *trusting* you. And that goes a long way toward getting them to be persuaded by you and to take the action you're advocating.

It's part of the winning communication style that I mentioned at the start of this exercise. Speak like this, and you'll quickly develop confidence that you're the kind of communicator who goes beyond the technical to accomplish your real goal: *influencing your audience positively.*

Exercise 70: Having a Conversation (With a Group)

Let's continue this dialogue in terms of speaking to large groups.

This is a daunting proposition for most people. I mentioned in Exercise 68 that **self-consciousness in front of large gatherings** is the most frequently named reason for performance anxiety. And it's true. I could probably buy an expensive car if I had a dollar for every time a client said to me: "I'm okay speaking to a few people or my team. But when it gets to be 100 people (or 200 or 400…the number given depends upon the individual), I get really anxious and develop stage fright."

And I always wonder why. Well, there's a reason I have that reaction. I sometimes joke with clients by asking them: "What do you think an actor will say if you told him or her that they had to speak in front of a thousand people? Answer: 'Can't we make it *two thousand*—can we find a big enough venue?'"

Because the truth is: *those 100 or 200 or 400 people are exactly the same ones you might chat with at the local coffee shop.* They don't pose any threat to you just because they're gathered together in a larger crowd. And their responses to you and what you're saying remain the same. It's not as if they mutate into a hive mentality when a critical mass is reached!

It's Evolution, Stupid. At the same time, I understand this problem in terms of evolution. I believe that stage fright is one of the ways we lag behind other aspects of our evolutionary development. I think that standing alone in front of 500 people might inwardly feel as though you're facing an invading tribe from the adjacent territory *all by yourself.* Just remember that this is an errant thought. No such thing is happening, and there's no danger for you here (the thought that triggers the fight-or-flight response).

In fact, when you come right down to it, speaking to a large group is a wonderful opportunity! It's your chance to get your message across once to all these people, rather than having five hundred different conversations!

So, don't fear it—welcome it. But remember everything I said in the previous exercise. For all the same reasons I named above, it's important that you have a *conversation* with people, even when the audience is sizable.

Being Yourself Is the Best Approach. You can think of it this way: the very best speakers don't sound any different when they're talking to one person or a thousand people. They're simply themselves. And so you must be, too. (Here's a trick that may help: don't think of talking to 'all those people.' Instead, imagine you're having a conversation with some friends in your living room.) In fact, it's very nearly true that for people to enjoy listening to you and *trusting* you, they need you to be conversational with them (rather than scholarly, stuffy, smug, or sounding like you're speaking from on-high). They want you to be yourself so they can be themselves!

And boy, what a confidence-builder it is when you can handle a large audience while remaining in control of everything you're saying and doing!

Exercise 71: Learning to Externalize What You Feel

It's time to release the inner actor in you! Note to same: now you need to *show* people what you're thinking and feeling.

If you're going to "connect with people through your personal brand" (which is the whole idea), your brand has to include tangible evidence of your own unique voice. Part of that is realizing that people aren't mind readers. They don't have a crystal ball that leads them straight into your mind.

Again, you have to show them the results of your thinking and feeling in demonstrable ways.

I can already hear your reaction: "But that's what I'm *telling* them in my presentation." (I know you're referring to the thinking part...but you're also imparting more of the feeling part than you're aware of.)

Another way to say that is, our uniquely human spoken language isn't enough.

Which brings us to the actor's art of *externalizing* what the character is all about.

The Way Actors Work Their Magic. Think about it. When you watch a movie or a television show or a play, the actors are all just reciting *word for word* what's in the script. Do you think that's enough for you to get an idea of who that character is and what they want? Of course not. You depend on the actor *externalizing the reality of that person* through the tools they have to do so: facial expressions, voice, body language and gestures, pacing, eye contact (or lack of it), movement on stage, psychological insight, silence, and any other subtle tools that that performer knows about and uses.

Here's an example: When Kay (Diane Keaton) asks Michael in *The Godfather, Part II* if he's responsible for his brother Fredo's death, the long *hesitation* Al Pacino employs before answering (with a lie) tells you how calculating, cold, and cruel this person really is. Just that actor's choice concerning pacing tells you something that the lines in the script simply can't.

Actors understand that for audiences to really get who the character is, they must play the *life* of the character that exists beyond the script! Watch any really good actors in a scene and you'll understand how that is what you're really watching and listening to. There's *a whole life* being portrayed by the actor as he or she is reciting their lines; and in the hands of an expert performer, the audience sees that person—that life being lived—unfold right in front of them.

The Lesson for Business Professionals. You, as a non-acting professional, need to use these same tools! If you don't, stakeholders will never get the full story from you. Oh, they will absorb the information and the data all right. But it's your *nonverbal communication* that alerts them to your belief in what you're saying, your passion, the immediacy of what you're advocating, your desire to get them on your side, the risks and dangers they may be facing through this deal, etc., etc.

This is a crucial difference between dramatic performance and business people giving speeches, presentations, and the rest. And really, it ought to be solved. Professionals in business often aren't aware that they have to externalize *who they are and what they mean* through the nonverbal tools I named above. In other words, going beyond the words they're using. What would they be aware that they need to do this? They haven't had the training or experience in dramatic art to understand it. But once they *do* understand it, their performing can reaching an entirely new level of influence.

The influence they're really hoping to achieve in this encounter. That's exactly why this exercise is included here.

Show and Tell at an Entirely New Level. So, consider this your quickie education. When you speak to others, allow yourself to *show* what you mean, don't just say the words. If you need to understand this concept better, look to your own life. When you're *not* in a formal business situation but are relaxed among friends or family or colleagues, you do all of this automatically. It's part of your human nature. When you're excited, angry, enthused, happy, confused, insistent, and experiencing any other strong emotional state, your body language, facial expressions, voice, and all the rest take on the coloration necessary to get your point across fully (including the emotional content). It's intuitive, and you never have to think about it.

Bring *that* person on stage in your business dealings. You'll be giving listeners what they really need to know about what you're saying. That essence always goes far beyond what can merely be said or shown on a chart. It includes—it's a huge part of it, actually—what is really being thought and intended and *shown* to listeners because now you're externalizing your thoughts and behavior so that they can be seen, heard, and felt. It's your *physical expression* of what's important for you to get across.

Just like the actor.

Exercise 72: How To Read People And Think On Your Feet

One of the skills of a consummate communicator is the ability to think on one's feet. After all, anyone can give a competent presentation or read from a spreadsheet provided they know their material and have practiced enough.

But what happens when challenging questions and objections raise their heads? Or suppose you're asked to reason your way through a thorny hypothetical situation when you thought you had all the bases covered?

If you can demonstrate your prowess in situations like these, you deserve a huge boost of self-confidence! Or, as Rudyard Kipling put it, in two lines from his famous poem "If—":

If you can think—and not make thoughts your aim;
And:
If you can talk with crowds and keep your virtue.

Why You Will Shine in Unforeseen Situations. Rather than fear situations which call upon you to marshal all your knowledge and experience, you should welcome them. For the fact is, these are precisely the occasions that prove your worth as a professional. If you can grapple with tough questions while retaining a mastery of your subject, then your persuasiveness, credibility, and influence with stakeholders will soar.

It's no wonder, then, that one of the principal tasks of a speech coach is to help presenters think on their feet.

So how is it accomplished? Like this: by bringing not only a fierce level of concentration to your task but also a high level of awareness of what's happening around you. Don't be like the oblivious speaker who buries his nose in his manuscript, or the green attorney who reads her entire opening statement from a yellow legal pad.

Instead, *be completely present and paying attention.* To speak powerfully in any situation is exactly like the major league baseball player who finds himself up against the league's best pitcher. Both you and he must bear down with 100% of your attention to what's coming your way.

Here are two ways you can achieve that level of focus-on-task so you can think on your feet and adapt to changing circumstances:

1. Pay attention with your whole being. Open yourself up completely to the nonverbal communication your audience is sending your way. In other words: make yourself one big receiving mechanism.

In the previous exercise, I discussed nonverbals and the need for you to externalize what you think and feel. But of course, your listeners are also sending out body language signals of their own based on their reactions and expectations that you should be paying attention to. And you should be picking them up! Yet how many speakers bury themselves in their content and are oblivious to these audience responses.

Don't let that be you! Watch and listen closely to how people are reacting to what you're saying. Pay attention not only to what they say in return, but how they sound when they say it. Mark any physical responses. *Especially make sure your antennae are out to receive their emotional reactions.* By responding in these ways, you'll be fully present to a degree you may not have imagined possible—and you'll pick up on things you would have missed otherwise. Listeners will not only be impressed; they'll be amazed because few public speakers are this attentive to the audience. Chalk up another mark of confidence for you!

2. Expect a reaction. Most of the time, listeners won't react visibly or audibly to what you're saying. Audiences are pre-conditioned to be passive and unresponsive. Even people who are intensely interested in your topic often won't show it outwardly. But you should speak as if you could get a reaction from anyone in the audience *any moment now.* And sometimes, you will.

Being that focused and ready will keep you fresh and responsive in real time. When you do get an externalized reaction from a listener or participant, you'll be able to respond to it instantly. Just as important, you'll be demonstrating an honest communication style that shows you're right there with stakeholders every step of the way.

Exercise 73: More Thinking On Your Feet: Impromptus

Ready to really challenge yourself in terms of thinking quickly while speaking? Use the exercise below. It's one I created for my coaching clients. I call it "One-Minute Impromptus."

ONE-MINUTE IMPROMPTUS

The task is simple but devilishly challenging. I tell the client he or she will have one minute to take notes on a subject I'll give them, before speaking for *one minute* on that topic. A stopwatch or timer on my smartphone keeps both of us honest.

Of course, I choose a topic related to the client's work or the type of interactions they perform on the job so the exercise is helpful for their professional life. For people who pitch business, routinely face tough audiences, or worry about their ability to respond quickly to unexpected challenges, One-Minute Impromptus is a natural skills- and confidence builder. (It's also a great exercise for my political clients who are facing debates and media interviews.)

Frequently, a client's first reaction to the exercise is that it's virtually impossible to do! It's interesting, for instance, how often in our first run-through of the exercise, he or she will say when the one-minute beep sounds: "But I didn't get to my topic yet!"

In Round 2, they always do better—realizing, for instance (and this is an essential point) that you need to make it clear to your listeners where you're headed *at the very start of your remarks*. You only have ONE MINUTE, after all, to a) introduce your topic, b) develop it somehow, c) give an example of it in action, and d) end strongly in a way that will stick with the listener.

Admittedly, that's a tall order when you're trying One Minute Impromptus for the first time and you've only had one minute to prepare! (As you can imagine, the exercise helps train your mind *how to think and organize your thoughts quickly*.) The client and I will often go through three, four, or even five or six run-throughs of the same one-minute talk, videotaping and debriefing each time. And it's always amazing how quickly the person learns how to achieve greater clarity and conciseness in that brutally short period of time.

If you have a need to think on your feet during meetings,

strategy sessions, working through a problem with a client, or tough questions following your presentations (and who doesn't?) you can build your confidence greatly with this exercise.

How to Play One-Minute Impromptus. Here's the simple rules of how you play the game:

1. **Write out at least a half-dozen topics beforehand and place them in an envelope.** The more they represent problem areas for you that you usually struggle with when you speak, the better. It's much safer to say to yourself when your smartphone beeps in a practice session, "But I didn't get to the topic yet!" than to come to that realization when you're actually speaking in public!

2. **Let a sufficient amount of time go by before you go back to your envelope with the topics.** Say, at least a week. By then, you'll have forgotten the challenging queries or thorny scenarios you wrote down. That's exactly what you want to happen. After all, you'll be simulating situations where *you don't know what's coming* from your audience in the way of questions and objections and you need to be able to respond in the moment.

3. **Now you have a nice supply of relevant, mega-challenging topics** as you wrestle with this tough but eye-opening exercise in learning how to think on your feet!

When you succeed in the real situations, your audience's confidence in you, and your own confidence in yourself, will both soar.

Exercise 74: Storytelling To Create An Emotional Response

Out of the fullness of the heart, the mouth speaks.
— Matthew 12:34

The truthful, inside story of almost any man's life—
if told modestly and without offending egotism—
is most entertaining. It is almost sure-fire
speech material.

— Dale Carnegie

Can I tell you a story? It's all about how you can captivate audiences so they're engaged, attuned to you emotionally, and eager to hear what you have to say.

Doesn't that sound like an essential part of speaking presence?

Chances are you already know that storytelling is a vital element of memorable public speaking. But, do you know how this approach works, as well as how to use it to effectively establish your personal brand and get through to listeners?

WHY STORIES MATTER

In the previous exercise, we looked at how to make your case in sixty seconds or less. And yes, even in that short amount of time, a story can come to your aid in terms of saying something that will stick. But stories aren't only helpful when you're under the speechwriting gun. Storytelling is one of the best tools you have for making people realize that what you're saying matters to their lives.

Simply put, speakers who are confident in their ability to reach audiences and demonstrate stage presence tell stories.

It's all part of effective performance. And telling stories is so ingrained in the human experience, that it certainly isn't limited to public speaking. Think of a parent (perhaps yourself) telling a child a story to teach him or her an important life lesson. Or consider *all* of Greek mythology; or the stories in the Bible; or the creation myths that are so central to indigenous cultures.

Stories go straight to listeners' hearts in ways that information delivered by other means can't equal. When I was studying acting in London, I played guitar and sang at a restaurant on weekends. An elderly couple often ate there, and seemed to enjoy the entertainment. One night, the woman had the waiter hand me a note she'd just written. It read, "Music hurts and heals. You tell the story, and you make it happen." Can you imagine how gratifying that felt?

And how true! The stories that these songs (some of which I'd written) were telling found a way to this woman's emotional center, in a way that I doubt a lecture ever would have done. As speakers, we nearly always focus—and sometimes obsess—on the information we think we need to get across. But there's a world of difference between handing an audience some statistics, and speaking with feeling about why any of it matters to them. In the end, what we're all most interested in is the story of our personal lives. Your job as speaker is to make clear that that's exactly why you're telling this story that impacts each individual listening to you.

GO FOR THE EMOTIONAL IMPACT

Data by itself usually doesn't carry the power to move an audience. However, telling a compelling story that relates those data to human motives—especially to the lives of your listeners—is what delivers the emotional impact you're looking for.

In other words, you need to tap into an audience's emotional responses. As Carmine Gallo says, "If you want to stand out in a sea of mediocre presentations, you must take emotional charge of your audience."[8] Want the scientific side to that argument? "The brain remembers the emotional components of an experience better than any other aspect."[9]

Here's something you must understand to be a speaker who moves audiences: every time you present, you're telling a story. You can call it a 'narrative' if you like. But you're always—or should be—creating a framework so that people can a) make sense of your data, and b) understand that information in terms of how it relates to their own lives and other people's lives. You might be talking about the most technical or conceptual issue imaginable. But if your audience is committed to it in their professional or personal lives, well then, there's usually a huge emotional payout for them in hearing you talk about it.

This is also where drama makes an entrance. Whichever narrative you're delivering will contain peaks and valleys in terms of pacing, intensity, immediacy, conflict, and other inherently dramatic components. And when the people in the story respond to this challenge and take action in the midst of conflict…that's drama! The mere delivery of information in most presentations can't touch this approach in terms of excitement, engagement, and the consuming thought, *"What happens next?"*

That last point is to remind you that you should tell your story in the present tense. Doing so puts listeners right there as the action unfolds. Like this:

"So here we are, sitting around the conference table,

stuck. It's 9:45 a.m. The client is coming at *noon*—and we STILL don't have a design that we think is good enough. We don't have anything that reflects our firm's reputation and leadership, and it's starting to make all of us very nervous. We can see the fear in each other's eyes.

Suddenly, I get an idea. It pops into my head, but I push it right back out. 'That's way too radical,' I think. Then a minute later, I say to myself: 'Wait a minute. What do we have to lose?'

So, I look at everybody, asking myself if I actually have the courage to propose what I'm thinking. Then before I even know I'm going to speak, I'm saying..."

As you can see from this example, stories have a natural forward momentum and drive. If your story is inherently compelling and told well, this forward movement can make the narrative unstoppable. Listeners become intensely interested in the moment-by-moment unfurling of events—especially, of course, if they don't know how it's going to end.

When was the last time you experienced that kind of momentum in a speaker's performance? If you felt it at all, she or he was an excellent storyteller.

HOW TO TAKE YOUR AUDIENCE ON A JOURNEY

In his 2012 TED Talk, screenwriter and director Andrew Stanton said, "We all love stories. We're born for them. Stories are from who we are. We all want affirmation that our lives have meaning."[10]

Another way to say this is, we recognize *ourselves* in stories. Stories resonate with us because we see ourselves in the events described. We identify with the reactions of the people in the story because we have those same responses. It's the same with your listeners: when they hear a story, their personal beliefs, values, and a lifetime of experiences come into play for them!

Conveying a Story's Essential Meaning. The next step in effective storytelling, is to *convey the story's essential meaning.* The information you convey to audiences as words, facts, and figures is not the essence of what you're getting at. It's incredibly easy to lose sight of this fact when you have a great amount of data to get across.

Listeners have no problem recognizing when you're using data to support your point. A well-told story, however, does something much more powerful, by saying, "This is what it all *means.*" Of course, the closer the events of the story are to your audience and their own experiences (or the organization's history), the more your story will affect them.

If you understand this point, and accept that *your audience is the center of everything as to why you're telling your story*, it will transform your influence as a communicator in public.

When you tell a story well, it's actually a story-within-a-story because it's really about those listening to you. It's actually about *their lives.* Remember, the important people in a room or auditorium are never you and the other presenters—the ones who matter are the listeners. Tell a story well, and in the end it's the audience that wins. In fact, if you were to create a headline for every one of your stories successfully told, it could read:

Audience Taken on Transformational Journey, Return as Heroes

Chris Anderson, curator of TED, says the following about talks that neglect to "frame" a topic well, including taking the audience on a journey:

> If a talk fails, it's almost always because the speaker didn't frame it correctly, misjudged the audience's level of interest, or neglected to tell a story. Even if the topic is important, random pontification without narrative is always deeply unsatisfying. There's no progression, and you don't feel that you're learning.[11]

For a skillful demonstration of weaving data into an interesting story, visit TED's own archive and watch Dr. Sandeep Jauhar's talk on "How Your Emotions Change the Shape of Your Heart."

Dr. Jauhar is able to introduce his topic, reveal his main points, and show how they relate to a lay audience, all within a narrative having to do with functional cardiology. It's an impressive feat!

ARE YOU GETTING AUDIENCES TO FEEL?

Compare that to all the speakers that use "soulless PowerPoint slides, facts, figures, and data...while neglecting to engage with audiences emotionally."[12] Equally important, compare it with your own presentations, and always ask yourself if you're using these pro forma tools while leaving out emotional engagement.

As theater professional and trial consultant David Ball reminds us, storytelling goes beyond informing listeners, "to make jurors [in our case, the audience] want to do what you want them to do. This is best achieved by storytelling, because a story influences not only what jurors think, but also what they feel. By influencing what jurors think and feel, you control what they want to do."[13]

After all, if one of your main tasks (and it should be) is to connect emotionally with listeners, why not use the emotion-rich technique of storytelling to do it? Brain scientists know that *every* decision—no matter how dry and *un*emotional it may seem—involves emotions. For instance, when a person's emotional center in the brain, their limbic system, is damaged by trauma or disease, the affected person is unable to make decisions. So, you make your own job of creating influence (and therefore confidence) much easier by establishing an emotional connection with the audience before they make any decisions about you and your topic. Stories pave your way to accomplishing this—smoothly, reliably, and swiftly.

So, don't ever just 'speak.' Create an emotional experience for the audience!

Exercise 75: 20 Reliable Ways to Relate to An Audience

To be a confident and effective communicator when speaking to stakeholders (or audiences generally), you have to go beyond merely delivering information. That's been a common theme throughout this book. Instead, you must try to get on listeners' wavelength *and stay there for the length of your remarks or presentation.*

Here are 20 reliable ways to connect with an audience for lasting influence. They represent a combination of strategy, tactics, and proven performance techniques.

1. **Get out from behind that lectern!** You may think of this as a podium (which is actually the platform you stand on). Anyway, you know that blocky thing located at center-stage, often with a microphone attached to it, that speakers stand behind? Apart from making you a static presence (think "statue"), a lectern is a physical barrier between you and those you're trying to reach! Instead, let audiences see all of you. Full-body communication like that is tremendously effective, as it literally help you *embody* what you're saying. It also helps put you at your ease since you're not forced to stand still. You can move with the flow and power of your ideas, leading to a feeling that you're speaking like yourself, and so giving you tremendous confidence.

2. **Wear a lapel mic that lets you move around.** Your performance needs to be as visually interesting as your slides! That means moving around the stage or room, and using full-body communication (see #1 immediately above).

3. **Make solid and realistic eye contact.** Forget the "rules" of how long you should look at one individual in the audience; pairing one statement with eye contact with one person; and all the rest. In terms of effective performance, it's artificial and phony. Instead, simply make a point of looking at everyone at some point, or at least to all sections of a large audience (since it will look to the people seated there like you're looking at *them*), for a normal amount of time.

4. **Get your body (and facial expressions) into the act.** There's an old B-movie from 1968 titled *They Saved Hitler's Brain*. Do not emulate this approach! You're not a brain in a bell-jar! Your body language and facial expressions are clues that you know what you're doing, you love doing it, and audiences can trust you (partly because you're *showing* them who you really are and what you believe in).

5. **Have a conversation with your audience.** As I've alluded to earlier in this book, The Age of Speechifying is dead. It gave up the ghost around 1896 with William Jennings Bryan's famous "Cross of Gold" speech. Even formal presentations are now informal. You're at your best when you're having a conversation with friends, which is what your listeners should sense they are.

6. **Use humor and a self-deprecating approach.** There will be plenty of time to drive home your serious points. Let the audience understand first that you're not full of yourself, that you're fun to be around. Self-deprecating humor can instantly help dispel the audience's natural feeling of "Who is this person, anyway, and why should I listen to him/her?" If you play it right, at least that sentiment can immediately be followed by the thought: "Oh, at least he or she doesn't take themselves too seriously." It's a pleasant response for an audience member to have, and can help boost your credibility. And, of course, when you see audiences reacting more positively to you, what does it do? — It boosts your confidence!

7. **Live in the world of your audience.** Remember Exercise 59, "The Two Solar Systems," in Chapter 12 on succeeding in social and business situations? That exercise emphasized that in any speaker's solar system, the audience is the sun and you are a planet revolving around it. This isn't just rhetoric. It's a reminder that you should always *conceive* and *deliver* your speech or remarks in terms of the audience's needs and desires. Doing so will automatically point you in the right direction in terms of giving listeners what they want and need.

8. **Use "you" and "we," rather than "I" and "me."** Another reminder from earlier in the book. Self-consciousness and the desire to do well will invariably leads you to focus on your success as a speaker. This is the wrong goal, and it will keep you busy carrying out the wrong activity! Instead, in everything you say and show, let the audience understand that they're the reason you're up there on stage. Inclusive language is a great way to do so.

9. **Ask frequent questions, including rhetorical questions.** Questions engage the audience directly, reminding them that they are an active partner in this enterprise. Your speech or remarks are all about *them*, after all, and it should sound that way.

    For instance, in a 20-minute speech, there will be at least a dozen times when you should ask your listeners a direct question. The questions can be substantive ones, of course (though the larger the audience, the less you should expect a verbalized response).

    But they can also be rhetorical questions, or questions

that are the type that I call "touching the audience." Here's how that sounds: "You've seen this problem many times in our industry, haven't you?" "Remember the new guidelines that the SEC published last year?" And, "You're all realtors, so I don't have to tell you what the housing market is like right now, do I?" As I said, you needn't expect answers. The idea is to incorporate listeners into your narrative. If nothing else, it's one way to wake them up when they suddenly hear that they've been asked a question!

10. **Include the three adult learning styles: (1) visual, (2) auditory, and (3) kinesthetic.** Some people learn best from what they see; others respond strongly to what they hear; and still others think in terms of physical, hands-on responses. Visual, auditory, and kinesthetic: these are the three adult learning styles. And though you may not be able to lead listeners in hands-on exercises, you *can* reach each of the above groups by using language that appeals to each learning style. So, you might say, respectively: "*See* what I mean?" "Do you *hear* what I'm asking?" and "Try to *get your hands around* this concept for a moment," and so on.

11. **Use shared cultural references.** Current remarks or behavior that have to do with culture can fly around the globe at warp speed via the web. You don't necessarily have to turn into an Internet influencer for this to happen. Every profession is a "small world," and people who are interested in the same things you are always have their antennae out. Pay attention to what's new, and especially what's current in your industry, sector, or favorite pastime.

Chances are someone will post what you say online (it might be you), and your influence may soar. Achieving that kind of reach should, of course, give you confidence.

12. **Tell stories.** See the previous exercise, #74—"Storytelling To Create An Emotional Response." If you're like most speakers, you may feel the need to present data on its own because it's important. But facts and figures are cold unfeeling things. Do you lose anything by *weaving* your data and other content into an engaging story that has people at the heart of it? You do not.

    It may be a very brief story you tell—hardly there. You can even create in instant story from a statistic. You could say, for instance, in remarks about the dangers of smoking: "Every year in the United States, 480,000 deaths occur due to cigarette smoking."[14] OR you can add right away: "Just how many people is that? Well, it's the equivalent of an Airbus A350 with a full manifest crashing *every day—with everyone aboard killed—*for 1,477 straight days." Saying *that* would certainly drive home that bare smoking death statistic, wouldn't it? The important thing here is that by adding human context to your data, you make it *human*. That allows listeners to relate to that statistic in terms of their own lives and experiences and those of their loved ones.

13. **Break up your talk.** When do people read emails, updates, reports, and other findings they are given? Whenever they have the time. But when you speak, they must listen to you in *real time*. That's an important consideration in getting listeners to follow along, understand, and stay with you.

People can only process information if you give them time to do so! (That's why people flying through their presentations because of nerves and adrenaline are ineffective.)

Each Segment of Your Talk Is a Mini-Presentation. Pace yourself. Think in terms of delivering your talk as segments that listeners can absorb as you're speaking, and retain afterwards. Here's an even more powerful way to think of it: your speech or presentation consists of sections, i.e., main points, *each of which should be a mini-presentation in itself.* It should have its own shape, feel, and inherently interesting points. If you think of your talk like that, you'll deliver each segment in a way that can be fully understood *and enjoyed*, before you go on to the *next* segment. If you don't do this, you run the risk of giving listeners an unending stream of same-sounding data that begins to pile up in their minds until they say, "That's it. The dumpster is full I can't absorb any more."

14. **Use concrete, specific language.** For the same reason as the previous point, your language should have maximum impact and be instantly absorbable. Remember what I said in Exercise 69: "The hard-hitting quality of Anglo-Saxon is what you want, not Latin's more ornate approach." For instance: "Inquire" (Latin) vs. "ask" (Anglo-Saxon); and "subsequent" (Latin) vs. "next" (Anglo). Notice how Anglo always use fewer letters to get its point across. Using simple, plain language is one way you can give your speech instant punch. Think Winston Churchill and virtually anything he said in one of his public speeches,

either in person or on the wireless. No wonder the British citizen thought of him as a bulldog!

15. **Speak visually.** That is, create "word-pictures." Our lives are now bathed in constant visual imagery from television, videos, streaming, and the web. This has made us *think visually*, so that now audiences expect information to contain a visual component. In addition to your slides and other visual aids, use spoken metaphors or descriptions (with details) to help listeners create a visual image in their own minds. Example: "I'd like you to imagine for a moment what our new campus will look like. See it in your mind's eye, based on the description I just gave you." BTW, "imagine" is a great helper-word for achieving this.

16. **Employ pauses.** Your audience needs to take a breath! The fight-or-flight hormone adrenaline may push you to speak more quickly than usual. After a surprisingly short amount of time, your audience will feel exhausted. Give them some breaks. Especially do so after you've said something important, so it has time to sink in. Two or three seconds is enough. Silence is golden, right?

17. **Get closer to listeners whenever possible.** I mean physically and literally. Go to both ends of the stage, come downstage closer to the audience, or roam up and down the aisles if that's possible. Even in a conference room, you can "stroll" along the sides of the table as you're speaking. You'll make the people sitting there feel more included than if you stayed at the far end of the room

next to the screen or TV monitor. Literal closeness leads to the metaphoric kind.

18. **Speak from notes.** Don't memorize or use a manuscript. Memorizing a speech or reading from a manuscript are both behaviors that keep you out of any moment-by-moment engagement with your audience. (When you memorize, you're actually in the past retrieving each segment of your talk.) Audiences expect even experts to have notes handy, and don't mind when they glance at them.

    But here's an extremely important point: don't be looking down at those notes when you're saying something important. And everything you say is important. Therefore, *if you're not looking at your audience, nothing should be coming out of your mouth.*

19. **Thou shalt not, on pain of death, read thy PowerPoint slides!** Your job is to amplify, support, explain, clarify, or put in context what's on the screen. That's the reason you're there in person, doing what a simple PowerPoint slide can never manage on its own.

20. **Move naturally to all the parts of the stage.** Every speaker knows about body language, but too few of them use the stage itself as a tool of physical expression. Watch exceptional performers on stage—no matter what their art form—and you'll understand the power of the stage itself.

Finally, think in terms of *strategic position*. For instance: where is the strongest point on stage to deliver your introduction, your most important idea, and your conclusion? Answer: it's always "down-center," closest to the audience and smack in the middle of their visual universe. Also, if you deliver each of your (3-5, no more) main points at different locations on stage—but still close to the audience—that will make it easier for listeners to keep the segments of your speech separate in their own minds and retain each of them afterwards.

Take a nice vacation to Greece if you want to become one of the statues that stand frozen in the sun all day, with no change of movement. Otherwise, I'll see you where the exciting speeches are taking place!

NOTES

1 Amy Cuddy, Presence, 26.

2 https://en.oxforddictionaries.com/definition/charisma.

3 Roger Ailes, You Are the Message (New York: Doubleday, 1988), 104-105.

4 Richard Dowis, The Lost Art of the Great Speech (New York: Amacom, 2000), 5.

5 Clients and others sometimes dispute my claim that they need to be vulnerable. "I swim with sharks," they'll say, or something similar. "If I show vulnerability, they'll tear me apart." The truth is, however, that stakeholders need to know you're vulnerable before they will sign on to what you're proposing. In other words, they need to see that you're human. Once they do, they can relate to you much better, identify you as one of them, and follow you. It's hard to be influenced by someone who's wearing a suit of medieval armor to protect himself or herself from the very people he or she is trying to reach!

6 Dowis, 89.

7 Ailes, 83.

8 Gallo, 144.

9 Op. cit., 145, quoting John Medina, molecular biologist, and author of Brain Rules (Seattle: Pear Press; 2d ed., 2014).

10 Andrew Stanton, "The Clues to a Great Story," TED 2012. https://www.ted.com/talks/andrew_stanton_the_clues_to_a_great_story#t-99643.

11 Chris Anderson, "How to Give a Killer Presentation."

12 Peter Guber, Tell to Win: Connect, Persuade, and Triumph with the Hidden Power of Stories (New York: Crown Business, 2011), vii, 9. Quoted in Gallo, 66.

13 David Ball, Theater Tips and Strategies for Jury Trials, 2d ed (South Bend, IN: NITA, 1997), 101.

14 https://archive.cdc.gov/www_cdc_gov/tobacco/data_statistics/fact_sheets/health_effects/tobacco_related_mortality/index.htm